Fighting Union Busters
in a Carolina Carpet Mill

Fighting Union Busters in a Carolina Carpet Mill

An Organizer's Memoir

PHIL COHEN

McFarland & Company, Inc., Publishers

Jefferson, North Carolina

Library of Congress Cataloguing-in-Publication Data

Names: Cohen, Phil, author.
Title: Fighting union busters in a Carolina carpet mill : an organizer's memoir / Phil Cohen.
Description: Jefferson, North Carolina : McFarland & Company, Inc., Publishers, 2020 | Includes index.
Identifiers: LCCN 2020034635 | ISBN 9781476683041 (paperback: acid free paper) ∞
ISBN 9781476641058 (ebook)
Subjects: LCSH: Cohen, Phil. | Mohawk Industries. | Workers United. | Rug and carpet industry—Employees—Labor unions—Organizing—North Carolina. | Union busting—North Carolina.
Classification: LCC HD6515.R95 C64 2020 | DDC 331.88/1776409756—dc23
LC record available at https://lccn.loc.gov/2020034635

British Library cataloguing data are available

ISBN (print) 978-1-4766-8304-1
ISBN (ebook) 978-1-4766-4105-8

Front cover image © 2020 Artem Orlyanskiy/Shutterstock

Printed in the United States of America

McFarland & Company, Inc., Publishers
Box 611, Jefferson, North Carolina 28640
www.mcfarlandpub.com

Acknowledgments

I express my deepest appreciation to Patricia Ford for her stunning artwork that helped bring both the campaign and this book to life. She also offered valuable insight as my editorial assistant.

If I were a factory worker, I would join a union.
—Franklin D. Roosevelt

Table of Contents

Table of Contents

Author's Note

This is a true story of my efforts to investigate and expose an illegal union-busting plot by Mohawk Industries at its Eden, North Carolina, carpet mill in 2017 and the resulting labor dispute that rocked a Fortune 500 company.

The names of Mohawk employees, hourly and management, have been changed. Personal details of certain witnesses have been altered. The names of Local 294-T Executive Board members and other people have not been changed.

Legal documents referenced herein are available on the NLRB website. Interviews with local union officers and witnesses were reconstructed from my notes.

Prologue

I've been a union member since 1974 and a player in the world of organized labor since 1980. I was chief steward at a bus garage for eight years, turning a worthless local into one that effectively represented workers. This led to my being hired as a lead organizer and troubleshooter by the Amalgamated Clothing and Textile Workers Union in 1988.

I took to the field in the wake of a painful divorce. For six years, my exploits were seasoned with a succession of wild, beautiful, crazy women … a lifestyle that might have been the envy of most guys, if one factored out the heartache and instability that came with it.

But I always kept my balance and wits about me while on assignment. I'd emerged from a rough blue-collar background, knew the streets and how to handle myself. It earned the trust of union members, and perhaps more important, put me in a position to pass on what life had taught me. I became one of the union's key assets in fighting professional union busters, negotiating first contracts, and rehabilitating troubled locals.

On November 17, 1993, I was home in North Carolina for the weekend and went to a party. It was a pleasant evening and most of the guests were outdoors. The first thing I noticed was an attractive woman sitting in a chair beside the house, crying hysterically. One of my former girlfriends sat beside her, trying to offer comfort. Melanie loved to talk and give advice but listening wasn't her strong suit. Everything she said only served to heighten the frenzy.

I put my hand on Melanie's shoulder and said, "How about giving me a shot."

She paused in her litany of self-help rhetoric, glanced up at me and gracefully exited. I took her seat. The woman beside me was named Patricia and we'd briefly become acquainted at a party the previous year. We'd chatted for half an hour about space travel and government conspiracies, while I bookmarked her perfect derriere in snug jeans for future reference.

Prologue

But she was currently in the midst of a total meltdown. All I wanted was to find a way to get through and ease her misery.

"I'm a terrible person," she wailed through the ocean of tears flowing down her face. "I don't deserve anyone's help!"

I looked deep into her hazel eyes and asked "Why?"

"I broke up with someone three days ago." Her sobbing eased just enough to enunciate the words. "I packed all night long, and then totally trashed his place on my way out at dawn. I didn't even tell him I was leaving. I just drove and drove without stopping all the way back from Texas. Only a totally worthless piece of shit would do something like that."

Tears were still streaming from Patricia's eyes, but she seemed to be stabilizing and becoming more coherent. Her boyfriend was a recovering alcoholic who'd promised to remain sober if she moved in with him. She was just getting over another relationship with a substance abuser. One night she returned home to find him sitting in a chair, passed out next to an open case of beer with empties scattered across the floor.

Her volume rose and a fresh wave of tears tumbled down her cheeks. "Three nights ago I just couldn't take it anymore!!!"

"You're not a bad person," I said. "You just got pushed too far. Let's go for a walk."

We strolled down rural pathways for hours. Alcohol had been Patricia's constant companion since early childhood. Her father was a drunk who beat her mercilessly. She'd become a heavy drinker in college.

"I felt like I just wanted to die once I got back," she said. "I had nowhere else to go, so I went to my parents' house. I had a long talk with God, and decided that instead of killing myself, I'd NEVER let alcohol back into my life. Never, fucking never!!"

It was a cloudless night and the sky was illuminated by galaxies. I looked up and it felt like the heavens had opened and we were being embraced by angels.

"Wanna come home with me?" I asked.

Over the next fifteen years, free trade agreements made it impossible for domestic clothing and textile manufacturing to compete with third-world wages and working conditions. As plants shut, my union began organizing in other business sectors, changed its name to Workers United, and eventually became affiliated with Service Employees International Union.

In 2011, I retired from the labor movement at age sixty. For the next twelve months, I considered it my job to rest and recover from twenty-three years in the field. But I wasn't cut out for life in a recliner. I wrote a book about one of my campaigns, got a publishing deal, did a lot of press interviews and went on a book tour. By the fall of 2017, this flurry of new activity was winding down.

Meanwhile, the most anti-union president in our nation's history got himself elected and ushered in a new era for forces opposing workers' rights. The assault was spearheaded by the National Right to Work Committee, an organization funded by big business and right-wing fanatics. Their attorneys insert themselves into labor disputes across the country, using them as platforms to sponsor legislation that would dismantle protections enjoyed by American workers since 1935. For corporations resenting employee representation, it was now open season.

Patricia and I were standing in the kitchen one afternoon in October 2017. "I miss the action," I told her. "I'm starting to feel that itch again. I want a mission."

PART ONE

The Campaign

If you know the enemy and know yourself
You need not fear the result of a hundred battles
—Sun Tzu, *The Art of War*

CHAPTER 1

The Committee

On the afternoon of November 3, 2017, the message light on my landline was blinking. "You have ... one message ... from ... 336-3..." As soon as I heard the fourth number, I sensed it was going to be Anthony Coles, the union's Carolina director. I also knew he wasn't just calling to say "hello."

"Phil, this is Anthony. We got us a problem up here in Eden, maybe you could help us with. Give me a call at the office."

I immediately dialed and his secretary transferred the call. Anthony and I shared a long history. When we met in 1988, he was a barely active shop steward in a crumbling South Carolina local I'd been assigned to salvage. Within five minutes I recognized him as the person to train and mentor to become the local union's next president. Two years later he was hired by the Amalgamated Clothing and Textile Workers Union (ACTWU) as an organizer and became state director in the late 1990s.

"We got us this situation at the Karastan plant," said Anthony. "This group of *anti's* been circulating a decertification petition. They been running all over the plant getting signatures, and we know the company's behind it, but we need someone who can go up there and build a case with the Labor Board."

"I'm in."

I heard Anthony slowly exhale and felt a wave of relief pass over him. I asked when the *decert window* had opened and how long the petition had been in circulation. The window is a thirty day period shortly before a union contract expires. If thirty percent of hourly workers sign a petition to remove the union, an election is scheduled to determine its future. Federal law requires management to remain neutral during this process. The National Labor Relations Board will block an election if the union can prove company involvement. *Anti's* is common vernacular for anti-union employees.

Anthony told me the petition began circulating during early October and the signature threshold had been achieved.

"Please don't tell me the petition has already been filed," I said.

"I got a notice from the NLRB that it was filed two days ago."

The National Labor Relations Board is a regulatory agency overseeing relationships between unions and employers. It establishes and eliminates union locals based on election results governed by strict protocols.

"Why the fuck wasn't I sent in a month ago?" I asked with exasperation. "I could have probably shut this thing down from jump street."

Anthony explained that he'd finally received authorization following several frustrating weeks of making requests to the union's regional office in Atlanta. It had been hoped union attorneys could document illegal employer support for the decertification and file the necessary charges to block the election, but they hadn't gotten to first base. A successful investigation can only be conducted with boots on the ground and a desk at the union hall, earning the trust of bewildered workers who harbor the evidence but are afraid to come forward.

I asked who would be negotiating the new contract and learned that early negotiations had already transpired, and the agreement would take effect in January if we survived the current crisis. It was a Friday afternoon but I explained that due to personal obligations, I'd be unable to travel until Tuesday. I requested the phone numbers of *committee* members so I could begin my interviews over the phone.

Committee is an informal reference to a local union's elected officers comprising its executive board. Anthony provided three names, and I asked, "Tell me one person in this local I can trust with my life."

Without hesitating, Anthony replied it was Vice President Bill Pettigrew. He was far more experienced than the other officers, having spent several years on the road assisting with organizing campaigns. "He's kind of a redneck, and me and him sometimes don't see things eye to eye ... but he'll always have your back. Only other things I know are he's a confirmed bachelor and rides motorcycles."

"Can he keep his mouth shut? Can I tell him anything, and he keeps it to himself no matter what?"

"Yeah. I believe that much about him."

I inquired about the others. The director described them as "a good bunch of guys" with their hearts in the right place. But they'd never been through a fight like this.

I learned the Karastan plant manufactured rugs in Eden, North Carolina, had been union for seventy-nine years, and was one of the few surviving textile operations in Workers United. It became part of Fieldcrest's textile empire shortly after opening in the 1920s and was purchased in

Chapter 1. The Committee

1993 by Mohawk Industries—a Fortune 500 company with an international market in a variety of floor coverings. Karastan once employed seven hundred hourly workers and split its operation between two Eden facilities. Several years ago, there had been a major layoff and many senior union members had opted for an early retirement package.

In 2016, the business was restructured and new jobs created, filled by workers in their twenties and thirties. They knew nothing about the union's struggle to make this the highest-paid plant in Rockingham County, taking for granted rights and guarantees provided by the contract. Some of them were imports from a nonunion Mohawk facility, recently shut in Landrum, Georgia. Local 294-T represented 200 hourly workers, all housed at the main plant. Union membership stood at only forty percent, an open invitation for a hostile employer to exploit its weakness.

We got off the phone and I paced about the room for fifteen minutes, staring out my window at the bird feeder, wondering if I could still run a campaign at my age. I asked myself if I sensed danger. Decertification fights can get ugly. But a switch had been tripped in my head and I felt ready for whatever awaited me. I picked up the phone again and started with Local President Jeff Totten. It was 3:30 p.m. and his shift had ended.

"I been waiting for your call," he said. "Anthony told me he was going to try and get you. I met you at the conference in Atlanta last year, when you signed a copy of your book for me. You remember that?"

"Oh, sure," I lied. One of the challenges in my line of work is meeting far too many people to keep track of. It's hard knowing how to respond when being fondly remembered by someone you've utterly forgotten.

"Look, we got us a real mess up here," said Jeff. "All these crazy peoples been running all over the plant, trying to get everyone to sign this paper to get rid of the union. Now they know better than to come up on my job, but peoples be coming to me and telling about it."

I've learned from hard experience that it's impossible to conduct an investigation without controlling the interviews and keeping them focused. One must instinctively know when to give someone just enough room to vent, and then how to pull them back on track. I interjected and instructed Jeff, as I had countless witnesses before: I would ask a series of very specific questions and he needed to stay on-point by limiting his responses to what I was asking. Otherwise we could be on the phone for hours and I'd be no closer to building a case.

To put the grueling process in context, I offered Jeff a crash course in how the National Labor Relations Board functions and the pivotal role it would play in the coming weeks. The NLRB is a law enforcement agency of the United States government. It enforces the National Labor Relations Act, a statute governing how unions and companies interface. It's analogous to IRS jurisdiction over the tax code or FBI authority in criminal matters.

Workers have the right to circulate a petition to decertify a union. But under the law, it's illegal for companies to assist them. They're supposed to remain neutral. Even though I'd barely gotten my feet wet here, all my instincts told me this employer was neck-deep in the current situation. There's no way a group of anti's can be roaming all over the plant during working hours, coming into other people's departments with a petition, unless management is allowing it.

"What would happen if you left your work area to go around the plant signing union cards?" I asked Jeff.

"I'd get wrote up. But listen here, Daphne and Robin been talking all sorts of trash about the union, saying the plant's gonna shut if we don't get rid of it."

I apologized for cutting him off again, explaining there wasn't time for me to be polite if he wanted to save his local. We were attempting to build a case before the Labor Board. He needed to answer questions in the order asked, so I could quickly wrap my mind around the situation. "I've been doing this shit for thirty years. You don't know me and I don't expect you to trust me right off. Trust has to be earned over time. But right now, time is one thing we don't have. You gotta take a leap of faith, act like you trust me, follow my instructions, and let me prove myself as we go along. Because at this moment, I'm your last best hope."

"OK, I hears you, Phil. Anthony done already told me a lot about you."

I sighed inwardly. The first hurdle of making a quick insertion had been surmounted.

"Look, this shit is complicated. What you and I think should be important is irrelevant. All that matters is what the Labor Board thinks. The law is arbitrary. It's a game. You have to know how to play it and make it work for you."

I asked about Daphne and Robin and learned they were two of the primary individuals visiting employee work areas with the petition. Daphne was the formal *petitioner*. The law requires a decertification petition be signed by one hourly worker, as if it were their personal project. I explained that while it wasn't illegal for them to disparage the union to co-workers, it was off-limits for management, unless they remained within narrow guidelines.

Chapter 1. The Committee

My first move was to empirically document management knowledge of anti-union employees enjoying free access throughout the plant. While it's common sense that it couldn't possibly have been otherwise, the Labor Board holds unions to a very strict burden of proof. One of my initial challenges would be getting workers to understand that under our system of justice, the company was innocent until proven guilty, and common sense was not a legal principle.

Jeff asked what would happen if we got the proof and I told him we'd file charges with the NLRB. If the agency found sufficient evidence of management involvement, it would issue a complaint against the company: the equivalent of an indictment in criminal cases. The petition would be considered *tainted* and rendered moot.

"But the company's already got notices posted on their TV monitors, saying there's going to be an election to get rid of the union," Jeff interrupted. He explained management used television screens located in all the breakrooms and several departments to post messages to employees. I asked him to take a picture with his phone of the election notice and email it to me.

"Listen, if we file a strong set of charges, the Labor Board will block the election while they investigate," I told him. "If we win, there'll be no election. If you and some of the others can trust me, and follow my lead, we'll shut this thing down."

Having concluded the orientation, it was time to begin extracting evidence. Jeff was overflowing with a mixture of frustration regarding what had transpired during the past month and exhilaration over the prospect of finally being able to fight back, but with little comprehension of what that would actually entail. Buried within were things he'd witnessed that might become building blocks in our case. The process is much like mining for gold, sifting through pounds of rubble for a few nuggets. I asked if he knew of anyone who'd observed a member of management standing by and watching the anti's solicit signatures.

"I'll have to go back and ask about that," he responded. "But I did hear from a couple of folks that Margie Clemmons was going on jobs with the petition. She's like one of the department heads."

This was potentially far better than anything I'd imagined discovering during the first hour. Direct management solicitation is considered the capital offense of Labor Board violations during a decertification drive. The challenge would be in proving it. We needed to identify witnesses and convince them to travel with me to the NLRB field office in Winston-Salem, where they would provide a sworn affidavit. Anything short of that would be legally inadmissible hearsay.

Part One—The Campaign

Jeff offered the names of two witnesses: Natroy Reese and Derrick Moss.

"Can we set up a meeting with them at the union hall on Tuesday when they get off work at 3:00?" I asked. "Tell them there's no commitment, and for right now what they tell me is off the record. But I need to explain the process and the laws protecting their involvement. I'd also like the committee to be there."

When workers give an affidavit to the NLRB, they become protected witnesses of the United States government. There are strong prohibitions against employer retaliation. I'd been filing charges since 1990 and never lost a witness. *The Board* is prohibited from providing management with affidavits or even employee names, allowed only to discuss the kind of evidence they've been receiving. Witnesses remain anonymous unless the company appeals a complaint and a trial ensues in federal court.

"So you think we might end up in court?" asked Jeff.

"Not likely. When we get a good enough complaint in a decert, the company usually cuts its losses, enters into a settlement with the government, and moves on. In all my decert cases, only one company appealed, and we won. But if it did come to that, think of how much protection a witness who testifies under oath before a federal judge would have. What else you got?"

The local president once again took me by surprise. During late September, management had taken a hand-picked group of employees to visit one of their nonunion facilities. Several days later, these individuals began circulating the petition. Jeff didn't know all the names but I explained this could be easily remedied with an information request that management would be legally required to answer.

Jeff abruptly changed the subject and discussed a leaflet written by Anthony a couple of weeks before addressing the decertification effort. It had been left for employees on breakroom tables until a woman from Human Resources collected and disposed of them.

"That won't make or break our case, but we'll use it," I replied. "We'll need witnesses who saw her do it. Tell me more about Daphne. What's her job?"

Daphne worked as an assistant weaver in the Aviation Department, where the company manufactured airline carpeting. She filled in on the other weavers' breaks. I asked if Jeff knew of additional people working in departments other than Aviation, who saw Daphne in their work area getting signatures. He provided three more names.

"Like I said, time is one thing we don't have. The Labor Board is right

14

now in the process of setting up an election based on an uncontested petition. We got to hit the ground running and go from zero to sixty in five seconds flat."

I outlined a schedule for the coming week. I'd interview the first witnesses on Tuesday afternoon, accompanied by the committee to provide a familiar backdrop. Afterward, the local officers would join me for our first strategy meeting. We'd schedule *shift meetings* for Wednesday and Thursday. I'd write a leaflet containing a meeting announcement and email it to the union hall for copying. It would be ready for pickup on Monday afternoon, with distribution commencing at the plant gates that evening. Like most large textile mills, Mohawk ran a seven shift operation that required that union meetings be split into multiple sessions. It was imperative to engage the rank-and-file in our quest for viable witnesses.

"Well look," Jeff countered, "the way we usually do it is, I put up a posting on the union bulletin board in the plant, after it gets approved by management."

"And how many people show up? We're at war now, and we got to do things different. Besides, what I write ain't gonna get the company's approval."

"OK, I'm with you, Phil. I got you covered. Just tell me whatever you need."

It was after 6:00 on Friday evening and I decided to let other calls wait until the weekend.

I allowed myself to ease into Saturday. The next week I'd be scrambling like a madman. There was no need to get frayed around the edges until necessary. After breakfast, I spent a couple of hours editing wildlife photos taken on my rural property that summer, then went online to learn more about my new enemies.

Mohawk Industries is a sprawling conglomerate with plants throughout the United States and fifteen foreign countries, having assimilated thirty-four companies over the years. Their corporate office is in Calhoun, Georgia. The Karastan plant began selling rugs and carpets in 1928, developing a reputation for emulating the creative detail of hand-woven products. It was the only union plant in Mohawk's empire.

I placed a call to Mill Chair Darnell Meadors around noon, got his voicemail and left a message. Local 294-T was structured like an old-style textile local. The president was chief administrator, but the mill chair represented workers during the grievance process.

Vice President Bill Pettigrew answered his phone. "What you say there, buddy?" His deep voice was laced with a trace of southern drawl. "I been expecting your call."

I provided similar introductions to myself and the project as those given Jeff. I could tell this guy caught on quickly and had game. He'd worked at the plant for forty-two years, during which he'd been on and off the committee.

"The vice president's spot had been vacant for some time," he told me. "When all this shit started going on back in October, Anthony recommended that the others appoint me acting vice president until the next elections. I guess they all figured we needed a white face on the committee if we was going to pull people together."

I began to pick his brain for evidence.

Bill began by explaining *the five minute rule*. If workers clock-in and go out on the floor more than five minutes before the shift begins, they're supposed to get written-up. But the anti's had been reporting early to get petition signatures and hadn't been disciplined. The National Labor Relations Act (NLRA) prohibits disparate enforcement of plant rules in favor of anti-union employees. I told him I'd request the company's *Kronos* (time clock) records to document this.

Bill didn't have much to offer regarding anti's having free run of the plant, so I asked if he had any knowledge of management solicitation.

"The last few days they had to get enough signatures.... Margie Clemmons and HR management were going around telling people to sign the petition. Margie was threatening people saying things like, 'you need to sign this petition.'

"Now let me tell you this. Two weeks ago, I called our plant manager, Justin Scarbrough, and left a message. I told him there were two girls, Daphne Little and Robin Stone, in the Mending Department with the petition, when they were supposed to be on their jobs. He never got back with me."

I requested more information about Robin and learned she worked in Quality Control. Though not in the *bargaining unit* (employees covered by the union contract), she wasn't considered management either. The NLRB defines management as those who both direct the workforce and have authority to issue discipline.

Bill was clearly animated but seemed to have sufficient discipline to remain on track. I allowed him space to shift focus, as surprise seemed to be the prevailing factor in this preamble to a campaign.

"Now, they transferred Daphne to third shift for a few nights, and she approached Jeanette Woods at the time clock as she was finishing up on second. Jeanette's a shop steward in Weaving. We used to go together. She got up in Daphne's face about the petition and this fellow from HR named Ray comes over to separate them. Daphne walks away, and Ray sticks around and keeps talking to Jeanette, telling her about the benefits of being nonunion and that she should sign the petition."

"That's the kind of stuff I'm looking for. Will Jeanette testify to that?"

Bill promised to speak with her and felt confident she'd participate. The discussion turned to *captive audience meetings*: a mainstay in every union campaign involving a possible election, either to certify a new local or eliminate an existing one. Management herds employees into propaganda meetings and attempts to walk the fine line regarding how the union can be legally discredited. This venue gives them the home-court advantage. The employer doesn't have to rely on voluntary offsite attendance.

Management had recently held employee meetings in the main breakroom to discuss the decertification petition. Workers were assigned to meetings scheduled for their department and shift. Bill offered highlights from the one he'd attended: Plant Manager Justin Scarbrough had discussed a Mohawk plant in Alabama where the union had been decertified a couple of years before, saying employees were better off after the decert, and promising, "Things won't change if we do the same." He was rebutting the warning in Anthony's leaflet that wages, benefits, and workers' rights were at risk.

A Human Resource manager, whom Bill referred to as Leslie, declared, "The union doesn't negotiate wages. We give that."

"I spoke up then," said Bill. "I told Justin, 'You know that ain't true. You and me done sat across the table from each other enough times arguing about wages.'"

I steered the vice president back to the topic of management's coercive solicitation of signatures. I explained the hearsay rules and our need to find witnesses willing to provide firsthand accounts.

"The best witness I know of so far is this woman who works in Mending named Annie Southerland. She's been talking in the plant that Margie tried to get her to sign more than once. I've been there over forty years and people come and tell me things. I've got to talk to her myself. Now, she ain't no union member, so all I can do is try."

Bill discussed a Cambodian woman named Bopha Soeur who worked in the same department. There were rumors Margie pulled her into an office and made her sign the petition. She barely spoke English and like many immigrants, was terrified of management. He also mentioned an employee who claimed she was solicited by Margie, Elise, and a supervisor.

I inquired about Elise and was perplexed when Bill responded that she was the Human Resource manager, since he had just referred to a woman named Leslie as being in that position.

"Leslie is from corporate," he told me. "She's been here at the plant every day since 'bout a month before the petition started going around. Elise Griffin is our plant HR manager."

I asked if he knew anything about the excursion to a nonunion plant just before the petition hit the shop floor. Bill had been in the parking lot that morning prior to his 7 a.m. shift-start and witnessed a small group of hourly employees and management discreetly boarding a van. He later found out "from people running their mouths" that their destination had been Pergo Laminated Flooring, a nonunion Mohawk plant in Garner, North Carolina. Bill had little information about what had transpired during the visit.

"They all been tight-lipped about that. But there's this woman named Candis Bailey who was in the group. She was real active taking the petition around for about a week but then she stopped. She lives with Maurice Wyatt, who's a shop steward. He told her that she either needed to quit this shit or move the hell out."

I asked if Candis would speak with me, and Bill suggested starting with her boyfriend.

During the conversation my caller ID had beeped. It was Darnell Meadors and I returned his call. I reviewed the overall project objectives and previous discussions, asking if he had anything to add.

"My brother Thomas is the vice mill chair. His supervisor told him there were two women in Mending."

I asked him to elaborate and learned that supervisor Ryan Lewis had informed Thomas that Daphne and another woman were busy soliciting signatures in the Mending Department. His brother had investigated and obtained what sounded like good eyewitness evidence.

"Now we filed a grievance about the plant rules not being enforced the same for everyone," said Darnell. "Not just this one incident, but everything that was going on."

A collective bargaining agreement (CBA) contains a grievance procedure to address alleged contract violations. When in-house resolution fails, the issue can be submitted to binding arbitration.

I explained to Darnell that while I appreciated his effort to take action, filing a grievance about something that's going to be included in Board charges isn't a good idea. The Labor Board is an overworked, underfunded government agency, under increased pressure since the election of Donald Trump. An agent will sometimes get a case off his desk when a grievance has already been filed by deferring it to arbitration. This procedure might serve to remedy contract issues, but not the underlying violations of federal law needed to get the petition dismissed. It didn't seem a likely scenario in a case of this magnitude, but I made a note to check with our lawyer.

"I'm sorry," said Darnell. "We didn't know what else to do, or who to ask."

"It's not your fault. You did your best based on what you knew. I'll fix it. Don't worry."

On Sunday I wrote a leaflet titled *"Emergency* Union Meetings" scheduled to accommodate the various shifts on Wednesday. Following the meeting announcement, it began:

ILLEGAL UNION BUSTING

Karastan management is engaged in an ***illegal plot*** to bust our union. We've all seen *management's little pets* running around the plant with decert petitions when they should have been at work. Some of us have even been directly approached by management with petitions.

This violates federal law. It is illegal union busting. It is illegal discrimination against the union. We will be filing charges with the National Labor Relations Board this week. **The feds will soon be crawling all over this company.**

KARASTAN'S MOTIVE

Total control over your lives
Cut wages and benefits
No representation if unjustly fired

Anything they say to the contrary is a lie. Without a union, their promises will mean nothing. (However, their *little pets* will be well taken care of.)

The Union is Here to Stay!

I emailed it to the Eden office for copying and distribution and opened a message with no subject heading from Jeff. He'd attached a photo of Mohawk's TV monitor posting:

National Labor Relations Board
NOTICE OF PETITION FOR ELECTION

This election gives you a choice:
Work together directly to resolve concerns by speaking for yourself
OR
Continue to have the union make decisions for you

Part One—The Campaign

Had there been any foreshadowing of what lay in store the coming week, I'd have arranged my life differently and driven to Eden that evening. But an old friend had resurfaced earlier that year. She was homeless and in poor health. I'd scheduled an appointment with the Social Security Administration on Monday afternoon to help her get disability benefits. I couldn't make her wait another two months for the next available opening.

CHAPTER 2

Meeting with Witnesses

Early Monday morning, Anthony faxed a *Notice of Appearance* to both the NLRB and management, designating me as the union's representative. At 9 a.m. I received a call from union attorney Ira Katz. He was also semi-retired but still served as General Counsel for the Southern Regional Joint Board of Workers United.

"I hear you've been assigned to the Mohawk case," he began. He spoke slowly and deliberately, as was his style.

"Just happened on Friday," I told him. "Long time. How you been?"

"I'm doing well, thank you. Have you filed charges and an offer of proof to block the election?"

"You got to be kidding me. I just got handed this."

"Well you need to file right away or the Board's going to schedule an election."

Ira informed me that not only was the complex array of paperwork due immediately, but the Board's Rules and Regulations Manual had been updated in 2014, placing far more stringent requirements on unions attempting to block an illegal decertification. The process had previously been very straightforward. If the union filed charges alleging *unfair labor practices* associated with the gathering of signatures, the election was put on hold while agents investigated. If the allegations were upheld, the petition was dismissed. If not, an election was scheduled. Under current policy, the charges had to be accompanied by a *REQUEST TO BLOCK* form, listing all witnesses with a summary of their testimony.

"Look, Ira, I'm not a fucking android. All I've got is pages full of scribbles in a legal pad. It will take me time to assemble this into a coherent case. What should I do?"

Ira suggested I attempt to negotiate an extension with the agent in charge, Sarah Schafhauser. He emailed the newly-legislated form.

I called Sarah and got her on the first try. I explained my late involvement and the quality of evidence that was emerging, requesting an extension until week's end. She promised to speak with her supervisor.

Part One—The Campaign

The next morning I followed-up with Sarah, confident my request for an extension would be granted. I considered most of the agents and attorneys at the NLRB's Region 11 to be friends and colleagues, relationships developed during the investigation of countless cases. I'd never wasted their time with frivolous allegations, and over ninety percent of my charges had been upheld.

I was taken aback by the limited response. All Sarah could tell me was that Board agents and attorneys would *agenda the petition* sometime the following day. She wouldn't know when until summoned by her supervisors. If my presentation wasn't in hand, they'd proceed as if the election was uncontested.

I had several hours before needing to leave for the initial meeting with witnesses in Eden. I opened my laptop and began assembling the case. The bare-bones simplicity required for NLRB charges actually makes their presentation more complicated and time consuming. Pages of barely legible notes have to be distilled into a series of single-sentence allegations, many of which embody multiple counts of the same violation:

> During late October, 2017, Department Head Margie Clemmons restrained and coerced employees in the exercise of their Section 7 Rights, by visiting employee work areas for the purpose of soliciting signatures on a decertification petition, coercing and threatening those who refused to sign.

I faxed the charge to Sarah with a note promising an offer of proof following my meetings. It was becoming apparent how much the playing field had changed since my last campaign.

I was running late but took a few minutes to email an information request to local management, asking for a list of participants in the mysterious journey to a nonunion facility. I also requested Kronos timecards for the last two weeks in October, to investigate the allegation that anti-union employees had been allowed to clock-in early to facilitate solicitation of signatures. The NLRB allows unions sweeping discovery rights in all matters pertaining to representation.

In a separate email, I requested that committee members be allowed off work on Wednesday afternoon and Thursday morning for shift meetings, citing the Union Leave provision in the contract.

I dressed and wistfully pulled my travel bags out of a closet. For twenty-three years I'd lived with partially packed suitcases at the foot of my bed. It felt like a celebratory ritual when I finally got to fully unpack six years before and put the bags in storage. I'd appeared for the union in arbitration since then and spoken at union conferences and other venues after my book was published but believed my road warrior days were behind me.

Eden is a small town in central North Carolina, just south of Virginia. Fortunately, it's only an hour's drive from my house. I'd have taken the assignment if it had been in Mississippi, but this location was a good break in regard to my transition back to the lifestyle. I'd purchased my final staff car upon retirement: a black Dodge Charger. I cranked the ignition and headed down a maze of two-lane roads leading to a familiar location, but unknown ordeals.

I parked in front of the Hampton Inn around 1 p.m. and grabbed a luggage cart. I always try to arrive at hotels before meetings. Over the years my travel kit became increasingly complex as my ability to sleep declined. I now carried a large box fan to drown out noise and my own bedding. Hotel sheets make me feel like I'm wrapped in plastic. There was a folding metal chair, providing a hard seat to accommodate a back injury sustained during martial arts training in my early twenties. A small travel alarm replaced the brightly lit hotel unit, and I never left home without a guitar. It usually takes me an hour to unpack and rearrange a room so I can be comfortable enough to partially triumph over insomnia. I refer to it as terraforming my environment.

I checked into the hotel with the appearance of a strange nomad on a yearlong journey, but my steel-eyed gaze made several businessmen joking in the lobby think better of making a remark.

I drove an additional few miles down Hwy. 14 toward the Carolinas/Virginia District office. It's a common misperception that the labor movement overlooked the South as being impossible to organize. We're somewhat analogous to the Knights Templar during the crusades. While the southern United States is the most hostile environment for unions in the industrialized world, we'd nonetheless carved out impenetrable strongholds in a number of locations. Our union once represented textile workers at several large Fieldcrest mills in Eden, and the Teamsters were present at a Miller Brewing facility. But that was before free trade agreements pushed manufacturing offshore, transforming our economy into high-tech at the top, service at the bottom, with a growing vacuum in between.

In all my years with the union, I'd never worked out of the Eden office, but had visited it countless times for staff meetings. The old one-story brick building was like a museum of labor history. Cheaply paneled walls were lined with photos and memorabilia from campaigns spanning several decades, and union locals long extinct due to plant closings.

I pulled open the double set of heavy glass doors and walked across vintage linoleum tiles to a small room where the office manager sat behind an opening that faced the lobby. Taina had been hired after my retirement and we barely knew each other. She initially came across as deadpan until one established a connection.

"I know you've already got your hands full," I told her, "but this isn't business as usual. It's a campaign and timing is everything. I'm gonna be hitting you with requests as this thing unfolds, and you'll need to drop everything and respond. Sorry to complicate your life, but that's how it has to be."

"OK," she answered in a monotone and handed me correspondence from the NLRB emailed to Anthony on November 2. It required the presence of union and company representatives at a hearing on November 13 to discuss and schedule an election.

"Next time," I told her, "please forward emails from the NLRB to me immediately."

"OK," she responded, as if I'd just informed her that I like mayonnaise on my sandwiches. My heart started pounding. I felt like a relief pitcher sent in during the ninth inning of a losing game.

I paced about the large meeting area, choosing my seat behind the central table in a horseshoe formation at the rear. I attuned myself to the environment and waited. The majority of employees worked first shift and folks would begin arriving shortly after 3 p.m.

A broad-shouldered man with a neatly trimmed white mustache was the first through the door. He wore jeans and a black sweatshirt, with a matching bandana tied around his head.

"I'm Bill Pettigrew," he said as we shook hands.

He was followed by the local president, a stocky man who, despite temperatures in the forties, was clad in a white T-shirt prominently displaying the Pittsburgh Steelers insignia and ball cap. Jeff was carrying his copy of my book.

Within a few minutes, we were joined by the Meadors brothers. Mill Chair Darnell was of average build, dressed in a light grey jacket and purple knit hat bearing the union's logo. Vice Mill Chair Thomas wore a black leather jacket hanging open over a black T-shirt. His uncovered head revealed curly white hair and he also sported a mustache.

All of the men were tall, with a no-nonsense demeanor about them. A yuppie from a sheltered life might have found them intimidating. We walked toward the back and took seats around the tables to await our first witness. I wondered if anyone would actually show up.

Chapter 2. Meeting with Witnesses

A short, heavyset woman entered the building and Taina directed her toward where we sat. She introduced herself as Gwen Broadnax and pulled up a chair directly across from me. She worked in Yarn Prep.

Union members at the Karastan plant were familiar with dispute resolution through grievance and arbitration, but I was ushering them into the totally alien world of presenting a case before the National Labor Relations Board. I began with a description of the agency, their rules of engagement, and the rights and protections afforded witnesses.

Everyone who met with me at the union hall would have an experience they wanted to get off their chest. The difficulty would be making them feel safe enough to turn it into a sworn affidavit before government agents. Part of this process involves helping them understand that the NLRB represents an authority far more powerful than management.

"The fact is, from the moment you raise your right hand and take an oath before an agent, you'll have more job security than ever before. In the unlikely event management figured out you were a witness, you'd have to screw up twice as bad before they'd fire you. I'd go the Board and claim retaliation against a witness and trust me, the company doesn't want to go there."

I turned to the three committee members I'd briefed on the phone. "Sorry. You're probably gonna hear this twenty times over the next few weeks."

"That's OK," said Darnell. "We all got a lot to learn here and it helps to hear it more than once."

I sensed Gwen's comfort level slowly increasing and began the interview. Daphne and Robin had approached her machine during October and spent several minutes unsuccessfully attempting to collect her signature before walking off. But Gwen couldn't place management on the scene. It was useful background material, but not nearly enough to sustain an allegation.

A short, slender man had entered the office a few minutes after Gwen and had inconspicuously taken a seat on one of the old couches near the door. I walked across the room to shake hands with Derrick Moss and led him toward our group in the back.

Derrick worked as a floor hand in Weaving and didn't require a lot of explanation or reassurance. He was eager to tell his story and described a several-day period during October when he'd been approached multiple times by Daphne and other anti-union employees. On one occasion, Robin had told him that they only needed seven more names on the petition. He was also unable to verify any of this had been observed by a supervisor. I played a long shot and asked if he'd ever been solicited by a member of management.

"Sometime after my last talk with Robin, Miss Margie calls me on the radio and tells me to come to her office. I got to admit I've always felt a bit intimidated by her."

"Why?"

"I don't know. Something about how she just comes across when she talks to me. Anyway, once I get there, she starts asking how I felt about the petition. I told her I didn't feel anything one way or the other. Miss Margie then says she really needed me to sign the petition and I should go to the front office and see Daphne, and come back to her office as soon as I signed. I told her I didn't want to, but I would."

When Derrick returned to Margie's office, he was instructed to "go out on the floor" and solicit an employee named Charles Wheeler, and then ask him to get signatures from his brother and sister. He admitted to following her orders.

"You got to understand how Miss Margie makes me feel. When she says jump, I jump."

This was our first smoking gun and I asked if Derrick would be willing to accompany me to the NLRB office in Winston-Salem the following week to provide a sworn affidavit. The young man needed no convincing. He felt shamed and angry over having been bullied into betraying his conscience and sought the redemption to be found in setting things straight.

I looked across the hall and saw a tall man with a fit build in the waiting area. He approached on his own as Derrick exited. Jeff leaned over and whispered that it was Maurice Wyatt, whose girlfriend had been on the Garner trip.

I walked Maurice through the preliminary questions. He'd been approached once on his job by Daphne but didn't observe anyone from management on the scene. I cut to the chase and asked about his girlfriend's participation in the field trip to the nonunion plant.

"Look, I don't mean to butt into your personal business, but as a shop steward, I'm sure you understand how important this is." I looked him in the eyes, seeking some sort of acknowledgment, but he remained poker-faced, so I reviewed what I already knew from the committee: Candis had been aggressively circulating the petition for a week but abruptly stopped after Maurice gave her an ultimatum. I asked if he could convince his partner to meet with me off-the-record to discuss what actually happened during the Garner expedition. Even if she was unwilling to come forward as a witness, the information would be invaluable.

Maurice said he'd already raised the subject with her and been told all they discussed was *The Mohawk Way*. I learned this was a program already active in other plants where employees provided input about how to improve operations. Candis claimed the petition was never brought up. I sensed he knew more than he was telling but there was no point in probing.

The executive board meeting began around 5 p.m. We were joined by recording secretary Tanya Pittrell, who pulled up a chair to observe and take notes.

"How we doin' so far?" asked Jeff.

"Derrick gave us some great stuff, but we're playing serious catch-up and got a lot of work to do in hurry."

"We been asking for help since this shit first hit the floor," Bill cut in. "We been telling Anthony that the union got to send someone in, or we ain't gonna have no union. Ira trying to conduct an investigation by phone from New Jersey ain't gonna do it!"

"I'm not gonna bullshit you. I should have been sent in sooner. But I'm here now. If y'all just roll with me, we can still get out in front of this. How did people react to the leaflet?"

Bill assured me we'd have "some folks" at the shift meetings. He said much of the leaflet's content probably went over their heads but they were relieved the union was finally taking action. "They really got a laugh how you're calling Daphne and them *little pets.*"

I explained this was the whole point. The anti's had been running around the plant for a month like they owned the place, conveying the potent image that these employees had suddenly risen to a level of authority and perhaps it would be safest to go along with them. The first thing we needed to do was cut them down to size and expose them for who they really were.

"I've been running decert campaigns for thirty years, and we've won every time. This ain't gonna be my first defeat. The company picked an unusual group to lead this decert. More often than not it's mostly guys ... who are kind of thug-like. I sometimes refer to them as the *goon squad.* But here it's mostly these ditzy women, so I came up with a more fitting name."

Bill discussed one of the male anti's who'd been on the Garner trip, an electrician named Elton Graves. They were once friends. The day after the excursion he approached Bill and said, "Don't worry, I'm not going to be part of it." A week later he was circulating the petition throughout the mill.

"Now I don't even talk to the man," said Bill. "Someone looks me in the eye and lies to me, I got no more use for them."

Jeff asked how many more witnesses were needed and if Derrick's testimony would be enough to prove the company was dirty. I responded that we'd barely scratched the surface. The Labor Board wasn't going to cancel an election because of one witness or just a couple of violations … especially with Trump in office. The NLRB is an agency of the federal government, ultimately answering to whatever administration is in Washington. I briefly shared my experiences fighting a decertification at the Kmart Distribution Center in Greensboro right after Bush took office in 2001. We had to jump through hoops of fire for nine months before the Board finally decided in our favor. And compared to Trump, Bush was a friend of labor.

"So what's the worst that can happen if we lose?" asked Bill. "Is the union just out or do we still have an election? There's a lot in there that may not be union members, but if it comes to an election, I believe they'll vote our way. They know what they got under that contract, and they don't want to lose it any more than I do."

I told him this might be true if the election were held the next day. But from the moment an election is scheduled, a company dominates the playing field. Management holds captive audience meetings in the breakroom and discreetly approaches workers on the floor, making unrealistic promises and threatening to close the plant if the union remains.

"I'm stuck outside the plant and y'all are stuck on your jobs. People are fickle and easy to sway. This election is based on a crooked petition and we need to shut it down now."

Darnell asked what we needed to do next.

"Let me start by saying this. You've heard the expression, 'too much of a good thing.' A person can eat too much food, or be involved with too many women. But when it comes to a legal case, there's no such thing as too much evidence. For every witness we produce, a management witness will tell a different story. Our word against theirs don't win a case. We need enough witnesses testifying about the same type of violations, multiple witnesses testifying about the same incidents, that it creates a wall of evidence the company can't climb over."

I was in the preliminary stage of educating committee members about matters that challenged their fundamental belief systems. Being right and everyone knowing it were irrelevant. Building a winning case in the current political environment would have been a daunting task even if we'd started a month earlier. If all we presented to the Board was one person testifying about Margie Clemmons soliciting signatures, upper management would deny it, but hedge their bets by claiming even if it were true, she was a rogue supervisor engaged in activities of which they had no knowledge. The case wouldn't go any further than that.

"But everybody knows that Daphne and Robin been out of their department, going up on people's jobs with the petition. Half the plant seen them. We even filed a grievance about it which the company denied. Don't that prove the company's behind it and letting them get away with breaking the plant rules?" asked Darnell with an edge of frustration in his voice.

I glanced around the U-shaped table arrangement, making eye contact with each of the men. I reiterated the underlying principle that our opinions counted for less than nothing. The only thing that mattered was convincing the Board.

I recounted how many times I'd been in similar situations. Once a union rep develops a relationship with a Board agent, they tend to talk with him honestly, off the record. During such discussions, I'd been told time and again, "If you can't put management on the scene, we're not going to issue complaint." One of the many ironies in our legal system is you can send someone to death row on circumstantial evidence, but you can't get the NLRB to find a company guilty based on circumstantial evidence, no matter how compelling.

"Well that ain't right!" exclaimed Darnell.

I asked if he wanted to be right or win the case and save his union local. We needed to find witnesses who saw a member of management observing the anti's and doing nothing. Otherwise, the company would claim it had no knowledge and would have stopped the solicitation if it did. The Board would buy it, even if the investigating agents knew this was nonsense. They worked for an agency and had to follow its rules.

"Like I told you on the phone, there's no time to figure me out and decide if you trust me. As the Terminator said in his second movie, *Come with me if you want to live.*"

"You heard the man," said Bill. "We all need to go back in the plant and start talking to damn witnesses. Now, I got a few more names I can give you, and I'm working on more."

"Have you personally talked with all these people?" I asked.

"Not all of them. But they've told their friends, and near everyone in that plant talks to me."

Jeff pulled out the seniority list and provided the phone numbers of all potential witnesses we'd identified. I told the committee to give them my cell number, along with others who surfaced.

Our initial strategy session was winding down, but committee members lounged around the tables and continued talking. Bill offered his theory about what lay beneath the decert: In 2016, soft business conditions resulted in a temporary layoff, downsizing the workforce until sales recovered. Per the seniority article in the union contract, most of the new hires were sent out. Some of them were angry and upon returning, complained to co-workers that the layoff hadn't been fair, because they were better employees than individuals with decades of seniority who'd remained. Management saw and exploited an opportunity, spreading the message that at their nonunion plants, seniority carried little weight. When it came to a layoff or job opening, they prioritized things like education and personality traits. Daphne and everyone circulating the petition (with one exception) had only had a couple of years' seniority.

"In other words, Mohawk plays favorites at its other plants," said Darnell.

"You got it," I answered. "One more thing to keep in mind as we go forward: always expect the unexpected. Just when it seems like our strategy is falling into place, something will come out of left field and threaten to undermine everything. Don't let it rattle your cage. Stay focused and we'll deal with it."

The committee members began getting up and preparing to leave. On impulse, I asked them to stand together and pose for a photo. It was 7 p.m. but my day had barely started.

I returned to the hotel and booted my computer to check email. The subject of the top message was *RD Petition*.

Dear Mr. Cohn:

I hope this finds you well.

I represent the Company and Ms. Griffin forwarded your request to me. There is nothing afoot of which I am aware that requires a response to your request.

If you believe there is, please explain to me what it is and why you believe you are entitled to this information.

Regards
Fredrick Englehart

Nothing afoot except an illegal decert, motherfucker, I thought. But my first and only order of business was meeting the Board's deadline for an offer of proof supporting our charges.

The committee members (front row, from left): recording secretary Tonya Pitrell, president Jeff Totten and vice president Bill Pettigrew; (back row, from left): mill chair Darnell Meadors and vice mill chair Thomas Meadors.

Part One—The Campaign

I donned my leather jacket and walked several hundred yards to a conveniently located Ruby Tuesday. I knew better than to work all night on an empty stomach. I had a turkey burger and salad, emphasizing my haste and being served quickly. I exited into the cold night air, feeling so exhausted that I became disoriented and lost on what should have been a five-minute walk.

I sat at the desk and pulled my legal pad out of a cloth briefcase, examining thirty pages of scribbles that now had to be turned into a coherent legal document. I filled out the *REQUEST TO BLOCK* form, handwriting on hard copy, and began typing the supporting evidence:

Attachment to Request to Block
10-RD-209088

Mohawk Industries in Eden, North Carolina, has been represented by Workers United/SEIU, its Local 294-T (and its predecessor unions) for nearly eighty years, during which successive collective bargaining agreements have been in force.

The above-referenced petition is the direct result of an employer conceived and dominated decertification campaign. Members of management have actively participated in the collection of employee signatures.

I provided summaries of fifteen witnesses, ranging from one to four paragraphs. I hadn't spoken with most of them, and some of what the committee provided was based on second-hand information. But my gut told me the local leadership was credible. I felt reasonably confident that at least half of these folks would come forward. We'd only just begun to investigate. I had to shoot from the hip and hope for the best.

I finished my presentation at 11 p.m. and emailed it to myself, figuring I'd open and print it on a hotel computer, then fax it along with the hard-copy form to the Board. It would arrive in time for whenever they met on Wednesday.

I was able to access my email on one of two computers in the lobby but it wouldn't let me open the attachment. After several efforts, I tried the other computer with the same result. I attempted to troubleshoot both units with my limited tech knowledge. It was approaching midnight. I wondered if this was going to turn into a lost cause the day of my arrival, due to faulty hotel computers.

I asked the woman behind the front desk for assistance and she recommended additional measures to try with the computers. I returned to her a half hour later.

"This is a really urgent fax to the United States government." I gambled that this friendly, young black woman would be sympathetic and explained my mission.

"I'm not really supposed to do this," she said, "but if you come around the desk, I'll open the door to the manager's office and let you use his computer."

The document was printed and faxed within five minutes.

My response to exhaustion is getting wired rather than sleepy. It's a mixed-blessing survival mechanism dating back to my twenties as a night shift taxi driver in New York City. I endured a restless night but awoke with my wits about me and geared for action.

I once read that a healthy diet needs to include a sense of humor. I drank coffee in my room and then ate eggs and bacon fried in toxic oils from the hotel breakfast bar.

I called Sarah Schashauser and was relieved to get confirmation that my fax had arrived.

"My sources are credible and I'm confident that a good number of these witnesses will come forward. But given how quickly I had to put this together, I expect that some of the names on this list will be replaced by other witnesses we discover as we continue our investigation."

"That shouldn't be a problem."

I hung up and typed a reply to the company lawyer's email. Responding in-kind to his polite introduction it began, "Dear Mr. Englehart, I'm pleased to make your acquaintance." I reiterated and elaborated upon the detailed justification for the union's information request already provided to local management and concluded by stating:

> I am entitled to all of the recently requested information pursuant to Section 8(a)5 of the National Labor Relations Act, regardless of what you consider "afoot." The union is entitled to render its own interpretation.

I'd barely clicked *Send* when my cell rang and I noted a caller ID number that indicated an NLRB extension.

"My name is Neil Sagucio and I'm the agent in charge of the CA case you filed yesterday."

Charges against an employer are referred to as CA cases because they allege violations of Section 8(a) of the National Labor Relations Act. Charges against a union are referred to as CB cases because they allege violations of Section 8(b). Decertification petitions are assigned RD case numbers.

"What about the RD case?" I asked. "Is Sarah still in charge of that?"

"No. The charges are in response to the petition, so I'm going to be handling both. I'd like to start interviewing your witnesses as soon as possible."

I explained my late involvement and told him it was my policy to interview witnesses myself before producing them. He argued this probably wasn't necessary given his time constraints but I insisted.

I asked if all witnesses had to be presented in Winston-Salem or if he'd be able to come to the Eden union hall for some. The regional NLRB office was an hour away, and we were likely to get more cooperation if this accommodation could be made for those with second jobs or family responsibilities.

"I'll have to talk to my supervisor but I doubt it. The Board is unlikely to provide me with a travel budget."

I noted a further obstacle: getting the company to let groups of people who don't hold union office off work on union business every week. I suggested hedging our bets by requesting them off for only half a day, and arriving at noon. Neil found that reasonable. We scheduled my first group for the following Thursday and exchanged email addresses. He told me to inform management in writing that Darnell's grievance was being held in abeyance pending investigation of Board charges. Five minutes later I sent him the disputed information request and Jeff's photo of management's electronic posting.

It was early afternoon and I attired myself in a charcoal dress shirt, jeans, boots and black leather jacket for my first meetings with the rank-and-file. I drove past rows of small shopping centers and mobile home dealerships on both sides of the road, until reaching the more wooded outskirts of town and eventually the union hall parking lot.

I updated the committee until second shift workers began arriving shortly before 2 p.m. I walked among our members, introducing myself and shaking hands. It's usually difficult to get southern textile workers to attend union meetings. This is a very different culture than one finds in labor bastions up north. Jeff called the meeting to order once a dozen seats had been filled.

I arose from my chair and stood in front of the speaker's table. "My name is Phil Cohen and I'm Special Projects Coordinator for Workers United. I'm a specialist in fighting professional union busters and that's why the union sent me here. I'm your soldier in this fight. I'll stop at nothing to win and I'll die for you if necessary."

Every eye was fixed on me and the spaces between my words reverberated with silence. They didn't know me but could somehow sense I was dead serious. I provided a stripped-down version of the information given the committee, having only forty minutes before they left for work.

"Let me tell you something about union busting that I've learned from experience. The company is always behind it. It takes a professional to run a campaign. Does anyone here think that Daphne could have put this together on her own?"

Heads nodded and a few people chuckled under their breath.

"Does anyone here think it's a coincidence that the same small group that went on the trip to Garner ended up being the ones going around with the petition?"

"Hell, no," said a stocky man sitting in a front-row corner seat.

"Companies always look for a certain type of person to do their dirty work. They're usually insecure and deep down feel like they're nobody. All of a sudden they're granted special privileges, hobnobbing with management and their lawyers. The ringleaders are sometimes promised a bribe, either money under the table or a promotion. In their hearts they're selfish and easy to manipulate. But I'll tell you this. In half the cases I've done, within a year of our winning, the leader of the decert committee, the one who actually signed the petition, was gone. The company crumples them up and tosses them out like yesterday's newspaper. I can't say that's gonna happen here, just telling you what I've seen."

I used the remaining time to ask if anyone had relevant information or knew someone who did.

The committee and I had fifteen minutes to unwind between meetings. The majority of employees in the reduced workforce were on first shift, 7:00 a.m. to 3:00 p.m. There was a small second shift and a barely staffed third. The Aviation Department was divided into four twelve-hour shifts. The schedule of these day and night crews rotated each week.

The first shift meeting began with about twenty in attendance and was similar to the previous session. Several people raised hands when I asked for witnesses.

"Tell me everything you got," I implored them. "I'd rather hear stuff that's not relevant to the case than risk not hearing something that you don't think is important, but the Board would."

A short, slender black woman in a bulky grey coat moved from the center of the group to an end chair in the front row. "My name is Natroy and I work in Yarn Prep. Now I don't know nothing 'bout Daphne and them others coming up on people's jobs other than what I heard. But one day last month, Margie Clemmons came right up on my job and asked if I'd thought about signing the petition to get the union out."

"What did you tell her?"

"I told her I wasn't going to sign. But then she kept on, asking me if it was 'cause I was afraid to sign. I told her I wasn't afraid and she walked away."

"This is good stuff. Would you be willing to come with me to Winston-Salem next Thursday to give a statement?"

"Couldn't I just sign something here, and you bring it to them?"

I explained it didn't work that way. If someone didn't provide a sworn affidavit to a government agent, their statement wouldn't count as evidence. I'd try to get her off work on union leave and the union would pay *lost time* for hours missed. The witnesses would join me afterward for a good dinner. "Look, it'll be a hell of a lot more interesting than being at work, and you'll be part of exposing a corrupt scheme. You'll be talking about this to your grandkids."

"OK. I got to leave now and shop. My husband's expecting me. Just tell Jeff what time you want me."

I spoke with two more workers who'd been approached by Daphne and Robin on their jobs during working hours but couldn't place management on the scene. They would provide supporting context, but not a smoking gun.

"Do I hear a motion to adjourn?" I asked at 4:20. Everyone remained silent. "Look, under the bylaws, we can't adjourn unless someone makes a motion and it's seconded by two people. So if no one makes a motion, we're gonna have to sit here all night."

People laughed and a woman in the back raised her hand and made the motion.

Several new witnesses had been scheduled for interviews the following week and the committee had additional leads to investigate. The next meeting wasn't until 7:15 p.m. Taina approached our table and handed me an email from the NLRB that had arrived an hour before. It began:

Re: Mohawk Industries
Case 10-RD-209088

Dear Ms. Little, Mr. Englehart and Mr. Cohen:

This is to notify you that the above-captioned case will be held in abeyance pending the investigation of unfair labor practice charges in Case 10-CA-209405. Therefore the hearing scheduled for November 13, 2017 has been postponed indefinitely.

Chapter 2. Meeting with Witnesses

We'd scored a victory in round one. The election had been blocked because the Board found our initial presentation to be substantive. I presented the news to ecstatic committee members. My bold stance had borne early fruit and I was instantly catapulted to a new level of credibility. But now I had to deliver.

I asked the local officers to give me some silence to draft a leaflet, apologizing that it needed to start going out that evening at 11 p.m. to catch second shift on their way out. It was crucial that workers hear the news from us before management had an opportunity to control the spin.

I started writing but Jeff interrupted with a question. "So, do you want me to take pictures of whatever the company puts up on the TV monitors?"

"Yes," I answered with stress and exhaustion in my voice. "But if y'all want our message to go out first, you gotta give me some space."

Twenty minutes later, I emailed a leaflet to Taina titled *UNION BUST-ING PETITION PUT ON HOLD*, containing the message:

The decertification was management's idea. They formed a group of *little pets* to carry it out. (Who knows what these people were promised.) They were given free run of the plant to sign petitions during working hours. Members of management helped get the petition signed. **This violates federal law! It is illegal union busting!**

Taina handed me a printed leaflet, explaining she couldn't stick around to run copies because she had to pick up her kids. She pointed to the copy room. I figured we could take a few minutes to run copies after the evening meeting and made a quick visit to Ruby Tuesday to fortify myself for that effort.

Only two workers showed up from the sparsely staffed twelve-hour crew and it was a short, unproductive meeting. Everyone was eager to end their long day. I turned on the copy room lights and encountered a machine that reminded me of the helm on Starship *Enterprise*.

"Does anyone know how to turn this damn thing on?"

Bill and Jeff fumbled around with the controls for fifteen minutes until Bill found the switch in an unlikely location. The panel lit up as the enormous machine whirred to life, presenting what seemed like an undecipherable menu. I experimented with buttons and options and finally it began to spit out copies.

After twenty pages, it jammed. I followed the detailed emergency instructions on the screen, disemboweling the unit and pulling torn pages from its gears. Once I had it reassembled, I hit the resume button but nothing happened.

I repeated the procedure several times until the monstrosity obliged with several more copies before shutting down and repeating the error message. When its inner workings were again exposed, a frustrated Bill nudged me aside and began pushing and pulling on moving parts, rearranging their locations. I wondered if he was permanently destroying the copier but didn't really care at the moment. He closed it back up but the unit had nothing else to offer.

I called Taina on her cell, surprised and grateful this single mother with three small children answered at 9 p.m. "It's ok. I'll be over in a few minutes."

By 9:30, we were locking up the hall with leaflets in hand.

I encountered the hotel's night clerk upon entering the lobby and profusely thanked her for assisting me the previous night, adding that a union local might have otherwise been on its way to extinction. Once back in my room, I opened my computer for a final email check and discovered another letter from Fredrick Englehart:

> Once again, thank you for explaining your rationale for requesting information about the Garner trip. Your speculation about the trip is not correct, but I do appreciate your candor.
>
> Attached you will find the Company's complete response to your November 7 email request.
>
> Regards,
>
> f

The company's attorney obviously relished the polite banter between opposing representatives in the legal world. He'd only furnished the required information to avoid providing further ammunition for the union's charges.

The next morning I emailed Elise, requesting Jeff Totten, Bill Pettigrew, Derrick Moss and Natroy Reese off work for union business the following Thursday at 11 a.m. to meet with Neil. The contract didn't require that the reason for union leave be specified. I was uncertain of the response.

Jeff and Bill had little to offer as eyewitnesses, management and petitioners having cut them both a wide berth. But they could provide an overview of events during October and document prior enforcement of plant rules that anti's had since been allowed to violate on a regular basis. Derrick and Natroy would represent a dramatic introduction to rank and file testimony, if they could remain calm and keep their stories straight.

Chapter 2. Meeting with Witnesses

Most Board agents are friendly and unimposing, but that doesn't prevent some workers from becoming intimidated when placed under oath by a federal investigator. Statements coherently offered at the union hall can become jumbled and fraught with memory lapses. Many years ago, I'd developed the practice of typing my interview notes. I send them to agents in advance, so they know where to probe if something is overlooked. A copy is also provided to witnesses with the advisory, "I typed my notes from our discussion to refresh your memory. It's possible I got something wrong. When we get there, just tell the truth."

I prepared my first set of witness summaries, with each person taking up half a page. The blanks would be filled in by the interviewer, resulting in multi-page affidavits. I then sent an email to Elise, requesting a plant tour on November 15 with Jeff. The parties were subject to an old textile contract providing limited access to the union representative, accompanied by management, and requiring justification:

> As the new union representative at your facility, I need to familiarize myself with the various work areas, both for general purposes of representation, and as part of my investigation regarding employee allegations about the RD petition.

A volley of phone calls from committee members and Neil interrupted my writing and the day began to slip away.

Several weeks earlier, I'd scheduled a radio interview on WCOM in Carrboro to discuss my book. Patricia was asked to join us in the studio to offer her perspective on sharing my tumultuous lifestyle. Program host Tana Hartman was intrigued by the notion of exploring this new campaign during the program. But as one phone call led to another, I wasn't even fully packed when it came time to leave Eden.

I was barreling down two-lane country roads five minutes after the program started and placed a call to the station. "Good. Welcome. We've got you on the air," said the host.

"OK. It's great to be here." I spoke into my cell as I careened around sharp curves at seventy miles per hour. "I expected to be in the studio but..."

Tana interrupted my review of the last few days to ask how I'd "gotten into this."

"Ya know, I'm from a blue-collar background. It wasn't a happy childhood to put it mildly. I left home when I was sixteen and just lied about my age and started working full time."

Discussing my life and work by phone as I returned from the field at breakneck speeds isn't something I would have planned, but it's exactly the sort of drama radio hosts live for.

Tana asked Patricia to describe how we'd met and been drawn together. The somewhat detailed account ended with, "You know the old saying. Girls who grow up in middle class homes just love a bad boy."

I had to stop at the bank afterward, and while pulling into the parking lot received a return call from a potential witness named Jerome Culp. He was agitated and spoke in run-on sentences without coming up for air.

"I was called into the office by my manager, Felix Perez, and he told me that he'd heard I was one of the ones going around with the petition and it had to stop immediately because it was against the plant rules and he'd write me up if I didn't stop."

He repeated the story several times before I found an opening to cut in. I thanked him for calling but explained his information not only didn't help our case but would actually hurt it. It sounded like this was one supervisor who'd actually done the right thing. We didn't have an obligation to present evidence that would help the company.

"No, what you say is all wrong! He didn't do the right thing. I never went around with the petition and accusing me false like that is harassment and you need to file charges about it!"

"That's not the kind of harassment the Labor Board is interested in and as I told you, it doesn't help our case. I called you because I was told you might have information about the people who were actually taking around the petition."

"I don't know nothing about that but I won't stand for being falsely accused and I want to know what you're going to do about it."

Forty-five minutes later I managed to get him off the phone, noting he was a loose cannon to be excluded from further efforts.

CHAPTER 3

Plant Tour

I spent Friday in my home office on the phone, talking with Neil and potential witnesses. Jeff emailed photos of several management responses to our leaflet, posted on their TV monitors. I sorted through them and sent what I considered most offensive to Neil:

> WHY IS THE UNION
> SO AFRAID OF A
> SECRET BALLOT ELECTION?
>
> Employees circulated a petition calling for a secret ballot election to decide on keeping the union.
>
> The right to petition for an election is legally protected, and the company would like to honor the people's choice for an election.

Hostile employers, under the guidance of professional union busters, cloak decertification elections in the in the guise of democracy and American free choice. It's perhaps the greatest sophistry in western civilization. A company-sponsored and coerced petition, leading to a self-serving election, is antithetical to their premise.

However, the rights of both parties to editorialize the process totter on a thin line between expressing an opinion and coercing the workforce. I doubted any of the recent postings would rise to the level of a violation, but they offered additional context. In mounting a successful charge, it helps to provide motive for the allegations by documenting widespread *union animus*.

While on the computer, I Googled Fredrick Englehart and visited his webpage. He had no doubt done the same with me. Beneath the large photo of a balding, middle-aged man in an expensive suit, projecting a smug and imposing demeanor, the resume began:

> Fredrick Englehart is senior counsel with Walter|Haverfield.... His expertise in labor law comes in part from a unique career path; Fred is a former union member

and former business agent of a San Francisco Teamsters local from which he has a withdrawal card.

His areas of "significant experience" included "union avoidance ... leads clients through the decertification process ... and union organizing attempts."

I'd dealt with several company lawyers over the years who had started out representing unions but ultimately switched sides in favor of more lucrative returns. I came to appreciate having them across the table. We spoke the same language, and they were able to help build bridges with employers who'd retained them to maintain smooth labor relations. But I'd never encountered a former union rep who went to law school and then became a union-buster. I wondered if something had disillusioned Fred, or if he'd simply sold out for the big money. He probably made more in an hour than laundry workers earn in a week. We did have one thing in common. We were both self-made men.

Weekends at home can be a mixed blessing for experienced organizers. The sense of invincibility and limitless energy crashes as one's body realizes there's no longer need for a sustained adrenaline rush.

After breakfast and some alone time on Saturday morning, I found Patricia on the computer in her office at the other end of the house. She turned to face me. "How do you feel?"

"Like roadkill."

"Well, you look really good," she replied, smiling up at me. "There's a light shining from your eyes. Being back in the field suits you."

I can't say we've had an easy relationship over the past two decades. But then, who does? It's natural to celebrate similarities and tolerate differences while dating. But once a couple attempts to weave their separate lives into a shared existence, the stakes go through the roof. Incompatibilities clash like animals fighting for turf and leave one hungry for personality traits found missing. But an underlying river of love and common values flowed between our subconscious minds that kept us bonded through it all.

There are similar challenges faced by union field staff and members of law enforcement, though one is to the left of center and the other to the right. We live and work in closed societies, whose members become the only ones that can understand our lives and what we go through. Neither career is supportive of enduring relationships.

But Patricia became a true soldier's companion. She never tried to compete with work for my attention or complained about long absences and burnout upon return. Instead she became part of my world, traveling to conferences, local union events, and on occasion leafleting beside me at plant gates.

Patricia is an illustrator and graphic artist. During the 1980s she was a rising star, working for a respected news organization. But when artwork went digital, she was unable to wrap her mind around computer programs and her life slowly unraveled. But she's been drawing labor cartoons for my campaigns since we got together.

Bill called on Sunday afternoon. "Sorry I didn't get with you earlier about this but I was tied up with things the last couple of days. We got this boy named Troy Craddock who drives a forklift, and he says that he was approached by one of the anti's named Roberto, and then Elise about the petition. Now he ain't no union member but he says he'll meet with you at the hall on Monday when he gets off work."

"You struck gold if he comes through ... tying the Human Resource director into this."

Bill went on to provide a wealth of background information. Roberto was Mexican. There were only a few people of Mexican heritage in the workforce, but they were all against the union. Another Hispanic employee named Mia Linares had played a prominent role in circulating the petition. Both of these individuals had been on the trip to Garner.

Two executives from the corporate Human Resource office had been in the plant "every damn day" since sometime in September. One was Leslie, a director with jurisdiction over numerous facilities. She was being assisted by a Mexican colleague named Ray, who'd devoted considerable time talking to the several Hispanics in the plant, successfully winning them over.

I asked if we could connect either of them to soliciting signatures and Bill assured me he was working on it. He then briefed me on his discussion with Annie Southerland, who confirmed that she'd been approached by Margie Clemmons several times about the petition. He explained that Annie was "real tight" with two black women in her work area named Lisa and Emily. They'd also been solicited by Margie during the same time period. The three women weren't union members but he was trying to convince them to at least meet with me at the union hall, so I could explain the process and importance of their testimony.

"Now that would be fuckin' solid platinum," I told him, explaining there were two types of witnesses: cumulative and corroborative. Thus far, we'd been lining up witnesses who could testify about the same types of violations: being solicited by management, and seeing anti's allowed to run around the plant. Cumulative testimony such as this establishes a pattern but in each case involves a separate incident that no one else saw.

"The knife to the jugular is corroborative witnesses ... people who all saw the same thing go down. Keep talking to these girls and get them to come down on Tuesday or Wednesday."

On Monday morning I received an email from Justin Scarbrough, confirming my plant visit for Wednesday at 1:15.

Jeff, Bill and Darnell joined me at the union hall after work that afternoon. I wanted the presence of familiar faces as I attempted to usher witnesses into an unfamiliar and intimidating process. A few minutes later, a tall, lanky young man entered the hall. I motioned him toward our table and he introduced himself as Troy Craddock. His gaunt, pock-marked face with deep-set eyes and muscular tattoo-laced arms gave him a rough appearance. But he listened patiently as I explained his rights and was politely soft spoken.

He began by complaining that Roberto had been pursuing him after work, calling his cell and showing up at his house. "I got no idea where he got my number and address. I know I never gave it to him. Then a couple of weeks ago he stopped me on my forklift and asked me to sign the petition."

I asked if this occurred in Roberto's work area and if he was on break, which to some degree would have legitimized the encounter. Troy told me Roberto worked on the opposite side of the plant and his break was over.

"I told him I didn't want to sign the petition and he left. But right after, Elise Griffin from Human Resources walked up and asked me if I'd thought about signing the petition. She said they only needed a few more signatures and we could have an election. She kept trying to convince me for a few minutes and then walked off."

I explained the importance of his testimony but that it would require giving an affidavit in Winston-Salem to put it on the record. Troy said he couldn't do it because he was a single father with "two young'uns" and needed to return home immediately after work. I went out on a limb and asked if he would provide a statement to an agent who met him at the union hall right after work. Troy asked a few questions and finally agreed to something I could only hope to deliver.

I interviewed two additional witnesses who'd been approached by

Daphne and Robin on their jobs but couldn't directly implicate management. The local officers and I remained at the hall for another two hours, exploring new leads and just hanging out. I was quickly developing affection and respect for these guys. They were the sort of rough-cut, big hearted people I felt most comfortable with. They'd hit the ground running as asked and were devoting most of their afternoons to the case. This was no small effort for people who awoke at 5 a.m. to spend eight hours on their feet in a factory.

Bill apologized for not contacting me immediately after speaking with Troy the previous Friday but explained he was an "outlaw biker" in his personal life and rode with a club that often held meetings or attended rallies on weekends.

The next morning, I discussed our first affiants with Neil from my home office, and was told he'd be assisted by a colleague named Brent Kensey. Four witnesses split between two agents heralded a manageable schedule on Thursday.

I returned to Eden for a meeting with two second shift witnesses at 1:30. The first offered further evidence of petitioners enjoying free run of the plant, but without documenting management awareness. She exited fifteen minutes later and her seat was taken by a slender woman appearing to be in her early sixties.

Jeanette Woods was shop steward on her shift in Weaving, and one of Bill's several former girlfriends at the mill. Her account of the captive audience meeting on second shift was similar to reports from the day crew, including the presence of still-mysterious Human Resource personalities Leslie and Ray.

"One night a couple of weeks ago, Daphne came up on my job and tried to get me to sign the petition. I guess she didn't know I was a steward because she usually works on first shift, but they'd given her a temporary transfer to third. So there she was, on my job thirty minutes before her shift begins."

A half-hour later, Jeanette was at the time clock punching out and encountered Daphne punching in for her third shift assignment. She resumed her solicitation of Jeanette who became irate, telling Daphne she "already had a choice not to be in the union, so who the hell did she think she was to try and take away my choice to be in the union."

This was observed by the Human Resource agent known only as Ray, who was standing about twenty feet away. Immediately after Daphne's departure, he approached Jeanette and asked what her problem was with not having a union. He emphasized that employees would be "better off" without a union and that the Eden mill was the only Mohawk plant that had one. I noted to myself that it was highly unusual for a corporate executive to be in a factory at 11 p.m.

A few minutes later, I was joined by the local officers and a vivacious woman named Leila Mangold. A broad smile creased her light brown complexion, framed by long black braids.

"It was about 12:30 or 12:45 that Daphne and Robin came into the Mending Department. Daphne had the petition on a clipboard. They went around asking everyone to sign."

Leila observed the activity for "fifteen or twenty minutes." She complained to her supervisor Felix Perez, who said it wasn't right and he'd do something about it. But several days later, she observed similar activity. Leila pointed out that Daphne and Robin worked in separate departments with different break schedules and questioned how they could have both been in Mending at the same time.

The outspoken mender was another worker who'd chosen not to translate her union support into membership. But that was for another day. At this point my entire focus was on winning the case and I didn't want to alienate potential witnesses.

A tall, muscular man in his early thirties had been waiting patiently on the couch. He introduced himself as Lonnie Wheeler from the Weaving Department, yet another nonmember coming forward on the union's behalf.

He'd witnessed Daphne, Robin and Roberto soliciting at various times of day on multiple occasions, adding to a compelling array of circumstantial evidence that on its own would be unconvincing to the Board. But he did offer an intriguing yet frustrating lead: his sister Tina had been solicited on several occasions by Elise, Margie and Leslie, but had no interest in coming forward.

Lonnie was articulate and I could sense an underlying level-headed maturity. He was the kind of person I look for in developing leadership, but that couldn't happen unless he signed a card. He exited the hall, followed by Taina, while committee members and I remained. All of the day's witnesses had agreed to travel with me to Winston.

"I'm learning a lot from you every day," said Darnell.

"That's because you don't show up thinking you've got it all figured out, and waste time arguing about things you've never done. You got no idea how many locals have at least one person on the committee who does that. In this situation it would be fatal." I paused for a moment. "You seem to have figured out that the first step on the journey to wisdom is saying, *I don't know."*

Jeff looked up from texting on his phone. "Can I ask something?" I nodded and he continued.

The local president offered his opinion from the perspective of common sense. We'd just interviewed two witnesses who'd observed anti-union petitioners in their department on multiple occasions at different times of day. It was impossible they could have all been on break every time. Supervisors are aware when employees aren't running their jobs and it results in discipline.

"So why not here?" asked a frustrated Jeff. "Anyone can see the company's up to something."

"It doesn't matter what *anyone can see*," I said, addressing the group. I pointed out that Neil was an experienced agent and the scheme would be equally obvious to him once he began taking affidavits. But he worked for the government and his hands were tied by their regulations. I realized it was going to take more work to hammer in the realities of how the system works: that truth, unsupported by the rules of evidence, is meaningless. I decided to broaden their view by referencing *Highland Yarn Mills*, one of my cases in the mid-'90s.

The union had twice the evidence of anti's enjoying *free rein* within the plant than we currently had here. Some of them were twisting the arms of immigrant workers, telling them, "The big boss wants you to sign this." Though the agent in charge became a believer, he was emphatic that if we couldn't prove management witnessed at least some of these incidents, we'd lose even if he argued on our behalf. This was during the Clinton administration, with perhaps the most union-friendly Labor Board in our nation's history. I'd passed the ultimatum on to local union leadership. They investigated more thoroughly and we eventually won.

"There's people out there who've seen things they're not telling," I said. "Find them."

"Well, we all know what we got to do starting tomorrow," said Bill. "Look, I done talked to Annie and them other two girls again today. They say they'll be down the hall tomorrow evening, but won't be until after 4:00, because that's when their department gets off. They're still shaky so I'll get with them again in the morning."

I had no idea what kind of reception to expect as I dressed for my plant visit on Wednesday morning, reflecting on hostile encounters during previous decertification campaigns. Management sometimes couldn't resist the opportunity to go *mano-a-mano* with the union organizer. It never went well for them but I had to remain mindful of walking a very thin line.

I'd toured the Kmart Distribution Center in Greensboro during a 2002 decertification effort, shadowed by the plant manager and his assistant until they decided upon a pretext to evict me. We argued face-to-face for ten minutes and they threatened to call the police. "That's an excellent idea," I told them, reaching for my phone. "I'll call my press contacts and we'll have a regular three ring circus. Let's do it." The visit continued without further interruption.

I stood in front of the bathroom mirror, brushing my longish brown hair, then trimmed my beard and mustache, experiencing the inevitable moment of astonishment that they were now grey. Growing old has never been part of my game plan. There's nothing more tragic than a broken-down action junkie and I frequently wondered if I could avoid that fate. But it wouldn't be today.

I donned a charcoal grey business shirt, black khakis, my signature cowboy boots and leather jacket. I ate a sandwich with one hand while negotiating the curves of Hwy. 158, drove past the shopping strip on Hwy. 14, and turned left several miles before the hall. Within a few minutes, I received my first glimpse of downtown Eden, cruising slowly along its side streets of small businesses housed in antique buildings. I noted the old brick mill stretching on for blocks while turning into the front office parking lot.

I walked up a narrow staircase, entered the front office reception area and made my presence known by dialing an extension from the phone available to visitors. A short young woman with wavy black hair and glasses opened the door, introducing herself as Elise Griffin. I politely shook her hand and gazed into her eyes. She'd been cited by name in the recent charges and I was curious what she was actually feeling. Elise left me alone in the product showroom to wait for the plant manager.

Near the entrance was a conference table where I stripped off my jacket and sweatshirt. Before me was a large rectangular room, with artfully designed rugs hanging from the walls. The quality of several was so exquisite they could have been referred to as tapestries. It felt more like being in a museum than a corporate office as I strolled about.

"There you are. I got held up by something on my job," said Jeff, entering the room.

"Have you ever been on a plant tour?" I asked, knowing he'd only been president for two years.

Chapter 3. Plant Tour

"I can't remember there even having been a plant tour, long as I been here."

We only had a couple of minutes for me to fill him in on the basics. The most important aspect of our tour would be union presence. In the midst of the company's efforts to eliminate us, we were going to be in the plant as never before ... with leaflets and in person. It was a message we needed to spread throughout the workforce.

"I believe in leading by example," I told him. "A lot of folks are afraid and confused. I need to show them I'm not afraid, no matter what goes down today."

I requested Jeff guide me through areas where I could shake hands and make eye contact with the most people. But we had to be careful not to disrupt production, as that would give management the legal right to challenge my presence.

There was a polite knock on the opened door. A tall man with broad shoulders and a traditional businessman's haircut entered and introduced himself as Justin Scarbrough. He was dressed similar to me except for the footwear, sporting loafers instead of boots. A minute later he was joined by an assistant. I didn't sense hostility from either. We discussed the business and running schedule as if this was simply the introduction of a new union rep to the plant. I told them honestly that the walls of their showroom were covered with the most attractive products I'd ever seen manufactured in one of my facilities.

"You're looking at some of our high-end woolen rugs," said Justin. "We're very proud of them. They're specialty items, probably beyond the means of the average person, but we also have blended and synthetic consumer lines, and a growing presence in the aviation market."

"He means we make the carpets that go in airplanes," said Jeff. "You might not know this, but a few years back, Donald Trump bought $5 million worth of Karastan rugs for his mansions and private jets." He obviously shared Justin's pride in their workmanship, despite everything else that was going on.

I donned an orange safety vest, goggles and ear plugs as we walked through a corridor, heavy metal door, and down a winding flight of cement stairs into the production area. I asked Justin if their manufacturing process only included weaving, or if this was a *vertically integrated* operation. He responded that all of the yarn was currently outsourced, but the plant still had to wash and dye it before Yarn Prep wound it onto *warps* and *cones* for the weaving machines. Years ago, Karastan had produced its own yarn.

I inquired if the mill had been profitable during 2017.

"No, this is a difficult market. Used to be a person would buy an expensive rug, keep it for life and then pass it down to their kids. But now these young professionals want to refurnish their house every three years. They're less inclined to spend a lot of money on rugs they don't intend to keep. We're also facing increasing price pressure offshore where countries are learning our technology. But we're revisiting some of our production models and exploring new product lines, so we've got our fingers crossed."

I had the first impression of a man far more interested in running the plant than whether or not his workers were represented. It reinforced my belief that this was a corporately driven decertification. A good union organizer possesses the ability to exist entirely in the moment, and at the same time always be thinking ahead. At some point down the road, I would need relationships within the company to help facilitate closure of the dispute.

We walked across ancient wooden floors, down a series of broad, well-lit aisles. I was surprised by the level of hygiene as we entered the Weave Room. The computer-driven looms were several times larger and far quieter than their counterparts in cotton mills. Thousands of colored strands ran through machines long enough to fill two rooms in my house. The operators patrolled on platforms to keep things running smoothly. There were three types of looms in the department. A few machines were devoted to either wool or synthetic drop-rugs, and the rest to carpeting for homes and business.

Justin told me some of the looms had actually been invented and built from scratch at the plant, to accommodate their unique product requirements. "You won't find some of this equipment anywhere else in the world," he said.

At times I walked ahead with Jeff who introduced me to workers. I shook hands whether or not they appeared friendly and chatted briefly with folks who'd come to meetings. Periodically I dropped back to engage Justin. "This looks like one of the safest and most well-run plants I've ever walked through, in any industry," I told him, and then shifted the discussion to what I believed would be common ground.

I have a genuine interest in tapestries, stemming from an earlier time when I became enthralled with medieval art and music. I'd probably been the only New York taxi driver with this passion. I frequently visited the Cloisters to marvel at the Unicorn Tapestry and other works from that period. I cared nothing about their academic implications. They were simply beautiful and touched my soul. Patricia, on the other hand, had studied art history and fabrics in college and over the years passed her knowledge on to me. I in turn shared this with Justin, discussing a broader, historical context for his rugs.

I mentioned that during the Middle Ages, rows of children were positioned above hand operated looms, each controlling strands of yarn. They received instructions when to drop thread and when to pull back up, and weavers actually applied the color. Somehow through this process, the craft guilds produced some of the most intricate tapestries the world has ever seen.

The polite conversation didn't stop either of us from doing our jobs. During moments of distraction, I'd bolt up the three steps onto an operator's platform for a brief interaction. But evasions from my tail were short-lived, and I'd be politely asked to move on. We spoke briefly with Bill and Darnell, standing by their looms at opposite ends of the vast weaving operation.

Jeff steered us into Aviation, where entirely different looms produced various styles of airline carpeting. This was Daphne's work area, managed by Department Head Margie Clemmons. I was curious to have them pointed out and perhaps engage them, but neither was to be found.

Our party entered the Mending Department where I encountered women at long sewing tables. They painstakingly corrected minor imperfections, and seamlessly divided or combined rugs to fit customer specifications. Most of them had little formal education, but had risen to the level of skilled craftswomen, working slowly, one stitch at a time. I remained discreet when engaging someone from my growing list of witnesses in that area.

Jeff educated me about the various Yarn Prep operations. Some of the yarn coming from the dye house got wound on cylinders for warp threads that descended from the top of looms (taking the place of medieval children). He pointed to a pile of empties: huge metal rollers over six feet long, appearing to weigh several hundred pounds. The remaining thread was placed on comparatively small spools that fed yarn into looms from the side, generating the crisscross pattern of woven fabric. Jeff worked as a threader in a room between Yarn Prep and Weaving, stacking spools of yarn into frames that would be connected to looms by other employees.

We mounted the broad spiral of cement stairs back to the showroom. In the office corridors we crossed paths with one of the Human Resource executives mentioned by witnesses, and I was introduced to Leslie Taylor. She was middle-aged with an amiable southern persona blended with corporate polish. We chatted for ten minutes as two veteran business travelers, discussing the comforts of home versus sterile hotel environments.

"Nice to meet you," we smiled at each other and shook hands.

Jeff and I lingered by the doorway leading back to my parking area. "Why you so nice to her?" he asked. "Don't you know who she is?"

"Sure I do. But there's no reason to not be a gentleman unless provoked. Besides, I plan to beat them at the Board, not in personal confrontations."

I drove to the hall and spoke with Taina for a few minutes before Darnell arrived, followed by Bill and then Jeff.

"Are the three girls going to show up?" I asked Bill.

"I spoke with all three again today. I asked them to at least come down to the hall and meet Phil so he can explain to y'all about your rights and what this is all about. They said they'll be here. Now all we can do is wait."

We had an hour to kill and took our usual seats at the rear of the large room, in a space I now referred to as *my office*. The chair and tables were always arranged exactly as we left them. The Eden office was the union's administrative hub for the Carolinas and southern Virginia. Numerous locals in the vicinity once used it for meetings, before free-trade agreements and recessions took their toll. Now there were only two locals close enough for easy access.

I expressed my frustration at not having an opportunity to get a look at Daphne and requested more information about her.

"She's one of them that got hired two years ago," said Bill. "She was real pissed about being forced out during the layoff because of her seniority. She kept going around saying that she was a better worker than some of the senior ones that got to stay, and it wasn't fair."

The vice president described her as a fairly attractive woman in her early thirties, who had a history of "always stirring something up." She had to climb a ladder every day to get supplies and had complained the previous year about how male co-workers would gather around to admire her feminine charms. "What I thought to myself," said Bill, "was if she don't like it, why in the hell don't she quit wearing those tight fitting jeans and tank tops?"

He said management had previously considered her an annoyance, but she was now frequently seen out on the floor speaking with Elise, Margie, and Leslie from the corporate office.

I looked up and saw a tall, slender woman with long curly red hair enter the hall. "That there's Annie," whispered Bill. I walked up to introduce myself at the entrance and invited her to take a seat with us.

Chapter 3. Plant Tour

I spent half an hour carefully explaining her rights and protection under the law, and how an NLRB investigation works, before asking about her experiences. A floodgate opened and my note-taking could barely keep up.

"Margie comes up to my job and asks, 'Have you heard any good rumors?' I'm thinking to myself, she hasn't spoken to me once in nineteen years. She walks right by without even saying hello. Now the day before, Robin came into my department saying, 'We only need ten more signatures,' so I knew what Margie was talking about. I told her I wasn't signing and she stomped off mad."

"This is great stuff," I told her, "but please give me a moment to write it all down. I can't go that fast." I looked her in the eyes and nodded when ready.

The following day, Annie had observed Margie leading Bopha ("that little Cambodian girl") into her office to sign the petition. The department head then made a return visit to Annie's work table and spent ten minutes trying to solicit her signature. She asked if her friends Elma and Lisa would sign and Annie brushed her off by saying she'd have to ask them. Margie then walked to their nearby work stations and remained in Mending for most of the afternoon.

"That mechanic Elton also came on my job and told me the plant would shut if we didn't get the union out. He grabs a pen and says, 'Sign right now!'"

Annie paused at my request. I scribbled furiously but she jumped back in before my notes were complete.

"Margie came on my job and talked to me three times about the petition. I kept trying to change the subject but she kept right on. She said, 'I don't understand why Elma and Lisa won't sign. If you sign they probably will because they look up to you.' Two times Roberto came on my job saying 'We want the union out.'"

I told her this was the best testimony anyone had given me in thirty years and asked if she'd be willing to accompany me to Winston-Salem in two weeks to give a statement. She was welcome to choose the day. I'd either get her off work to be paid by the union, or drive her afterward, if she felt uncomfortable with the possibility of management guessing she was a witness. She remained uncertain.

Building a Labor Board case is as much about understanding human nature as legal expertise. Having a good union lawyer in the background is useful for second opinions and if necessary, filing briefs and motions before the NLRB's national office. But it takes a battle-scarred field agent with years on the ground to instinctively know how to persuade an individual without making them feeling pressured.

I explained to Annie that her testimony could make or break our case. Everyone's wages, seniority, and right to representation if fired were at stake, including hers. I acknowledged her fear of retaliation but assured her the Labor Board and union wouldn't let it happen.

I looked into her eyes. "I'm gonna say something to you now, not speaking for the union, but personal. If the company messes with you, they mess with me. If they find out you testified, and even look at you funny, they cross me. Believe me, no one in their right mind wants to go there."

Annie, lines etched on her beautiful face by hard times, sat in her first moments of silence since our discussion began. I sensed undercurrents of sensitivity and anxiety that were always with her. "I've never had no need for the union," she said. "But right now I'm afraid of losing my job if the union gets voted out. I'm more concerned for all the young ones in there and those that come after, being without a union. I can take care of myself but some of them can't."

I asked what she was going to do about it but Annie remained uncomfortable traveling to a government office in Winston-Salem.

"What if I could get a Board agent to meet you here at the union hall after work? Would you do that?"

Annie reflected on this for a few moments and agreed.

Two women had been waiting patiently on one of the couches for an hour. I apologized for the long wait and interviewed Lisa, followed by Elma. I reiterated my detailed description of the process to each in turn, and they corroborated Annie's testimony. Lisa had also been told by Margie that if she signed, the other two would follow suit. Elma said her sister worked in a nonunion plant. "I told Margie, 'When they give a raise, some gets it and some don't.'"

They both promised to join Annie if she met with an agent after work at the union hall.

I returned to the office at 11:00 a.m., after a restless night at the Hampton Inn, to greet the first witnesses I'd be presenting to the Board. Within a few minutes I was surrounded by Jeff, Bill, Natroy Reese and Derrick Moss. I took a few minutes to explain the art of testifying.

"Keep your answers short and on-point. If the agent asks what time it is, answer 11 o'clock. Don't go off a rant about how it's Thursday and the sun is shining. If he wants more information, he can always ask another question. If you put your foot in your mouth, you'll never be able to take it out."

I'd traveled to the Winston office countless times, but never coming from Eden, so I set my GPS. Bill and Natroy rode with me while Derrick accompanied Jeff in his white truck, plastered with Pittsburgh Steelers insignia. My phone led us down a confusing route of two-lane roads and side streets for an hour. I began to wonder if it had any idea where we were going. I used the drive to further prepare my passengers for the upcoming process.

There had been significant changes at the Board since my first case in 1989. The local field office was previously located in Winston-Salem's downtown federal building, entered only after passing through metal detectors and convincing stern security guards of one's legitimate business. But a number of years ago, their staff and budget had been slashed, and the agency was relocated to a small office complex on the outskirts of town. It looked more like a housing project than a business setting.

"It shows how much the government prioritizes the rights of workers," I told my passengers.

Witness protocols had become more stringent and increasingly formal. During the 1990s, union reps were allowed to sit with workers while affidavits were being taken. I'd once spent a day sitting with an agent and witnesses at a union hall with my five-year-old daughter on my knee. But those days were long past and workers were now sequestered with an agent in a private room. I tried to reassure my companions that most Board agents are fairly laid back and amiable. They wouldn't be very successful at eliciting information and taking statements if they weren't.

We entered the parking lot at 12:15 and I realized the years had blurred my orientation. I led my entourage through a disorganized array of drab three-story buildings, hoping my credibility as a seasoned veteran wasn't eroding with every step. The correct address finally presented itself. As we approached the thick glass door, I noted a sign prohibiting concealed weapons, instinctively tapping the .22 Magnum derringer in my trousers. I make good use of my permit. It's a dangerous world and I've seen it.

"Excuse me a minute," I told the group. "Gotta go back to the car for something." I've ignored the posting while shopping but wouldn't risk it at a government office.

We took the elevator to the second floor and I rang the NLRB's front door buzzer, stating my name and union affiliation through the intercom. The office manager let us in and announced our arrival.

We waited briefly inside the lobby. Another locked door opened and two young men wearing dress shirts and khakis emerged. "Hi, I'm Neil Sagucio," said the one in front, shaking my hand. He was short and slender, with a slightly olive complexion. He introduced Brent Kensey, nodding toward a taller but equally slender gentleman with hunched shoulders, who looked exhausted. I was surprised by their youth, guessing they were in their late twenties or early thirties. Neil led us to a hearing room not in use that day to serve as our waiting area.

We entered a small courtroom and I noted a plaque on the left wall designating it as the Paris Favors Hearing Room. A picture of a dignified black man in a suit hung beside it.

"Do you know who Paris Favors was?" I asked Neil.

"No, I don't," he said, shaking his head.

"He was an attorney assigned to this office. He was good people. We worked Highland Yarn and a lot of other cases together. I was up here one day and learned that he'd dropped dead from a heart attack at age forty-three."

I felt a genuine wave of emotion but realized the two agents had been small children when most of this unfolded. Neil looked at me like I was describing my relationship with George Washington.

Per my normal practice, I requested a meeting with the agents to update them on the progress of our investigation and schedule additional dates. It would serve as an opportunity to take their measure and begin building the relationships essential to a successful outcome. Neil requested a few minutes to make a phone call and promised to return for me.

We waited near the room's entrance, observing several professionally dressed people walking past, obviously agents and young enough to be my children. I was accustomed to appearing at this office with a reputation that preceded me. But I was getting the impression that most of the agents and lawyers I'd known had retired or passed, and today I was starting from scratch with a new group.

Neil led me through a locked door and down a hallway into his office. Brent was already seated and the three of us chatted for fifteen minutes to become acquainted.

"I recognize you," said Brent, "from your picture in the *Greensboro News & Record* a couple of months back, something about your book."

Well at least I'm not entirely unknown here, I thought.

I asked why their office stationery referred to Region 10 of the NLRB, as the Winston office had always been Region 11. Neil informed me they'd been placed under jurisdiction of the Atlanta office following additional budget cuts and were now Subregion 11 of Region 10.

"How long have you been doing this?" I asked.

"About five years. I was teaching Spanish but got laid off and jobs were hard to come by. I went back to school, got a degree in labor relations and ended up here."

I began discussing the workers interviewed during the past few days. We'd found four new witnesses with compelling testimony about direct management solicitation, some of it corroborated. Astonishingly, none of them were union members, adding to their credibility. These individuals weren't bound by loyalties that might be argued as motive to stretch the truth. Their affidavits could break the case wide open.

Unfortunately, they refused to travel to Winston-Salem and would only give statements at the union hall. One had family responsibilities and the others were very skittish, afraid to get off work early on union business and tip their hand to management.

"Why not bring them after work?" asked Neil. "I'll stay here as late as needed."

"Because they can't stay here as late as needed. These girls get up before dawn and work all day in a factory. They don't want to get home at 11 p.m. Look, I tried every option, and their position is final. This is a major case, and if you want their statements, you'll have to come to them."

"I'll take it up again with my supervisor. But they've cut our travel budget back to almost nothing."

Two dates were scheduled for the week after Thanksgiving, with the location of one remaining open. Neil surprised me by noting he was also the agent in charge of investigating *the CB charge* but they weren't in a rush. The charge against the employer took precedence because it was tied to an election, but at some point I'd need to file a position statement and schedule witnesses.

"What CB charge?" I asked.

"You mean you haven't gotten a copy?" Neil scrolled through his laptop for a few minutes. "Here it is. It was filed on October 27 and signed by Daphne."

I explained this was a week before I'd arrived and the Eden office had neglected to inform me. Neil glanced down at his computer and emailed it.

We returned to the hearing room. Jeff and Bill followed the agents to their respective offices. I set myself up at the attorney's table facing the raised judge's bench and took out my laptop. For the next few hours I would be utterly useless, other than making sure the witnesses felt comfortable and entertained. Neil had provided me the day's password to access the NLRB's internet server. There were fifteen characters, a random assembly of upper and lower case letters, numbers and symbols. It looked like the code needed to launch a nuclear strike. I spent thirty minutes deciphering the required protocols after typing it into the dialogue box.

I was accustomed to most affidavits taking a maximum of ninety minutes. I told Natroy and Derrick we should be on the road by 5:00 and enjoying dinner at Ruby Tuesday an hour later.

I responded to newly arrived emails, checked book sales and views of my photos on Flickr, revisiting my inbox in the hope there would be some new work to capture my attention. I paced about the corridors, shared war stories with the two witnesses, and pulled a sandwich from my briefcase at 3:00. Two hours later, Jeff and Bill still hadn't returned.

I reopened my computer and typed a leaflet titled, *LABOR BOARD UPDATE*, ending with a pre-holiday message:

BE THANKFUL

This Thanksgiving, in addition to the blessings in your personal life, be thankful for the following:

- You work at the highest paid plant in Rockingham County
- Wages and benefits are **guaranteed** under the union contract
- **You can't be fired unjustly** because of the union contract.
  (Under NC law, nonunion plants can fire people *at will*.)

Count your blessings and don't be tricked into giving them up.

At the bottom was displayed a slogan I'd coined during Highland Yarn and thereafter used at the end of every leaflet during a decert campaign: *The Union is Here to Stay!*

Natroy and Derrick finally got their turn at 5:30. Their testimony involved specific incidents, as opposed to an overview, so I figured we'd be stuck there for another hour. I hoped Derrick could offer a coherent account of being forced by Margie Clemmons to sign the petition, and then solicit co-workers.

Jeff complained about being hungry and I offered him a protein bar from my briefcase. He then climbed up on the judge's seat while I snapped pictures with my phone. It was 8 p.m. before the others returned with the agents.

"Did the witnesses sign the form for me to get a copy of their affidavits?" I asked.

"They've all been given copies of their statements, but I've instructed them not to show them to anyone, including you because you're not a lawyer."

"I've been presenting cases here since 1990," I said with frustration, "and there's never been a problem with me getting copies. I'm going to be filing briefs and position statements and need the affidavits to cite."

"I'm sorry but you're not a lawyer and that's how we're going to handle it."

The witnesses stood beside my car in the parking lot at 8:30 and handed over their affidavits. The temperature had dropped into the thirties and we were all cold and exhausted. Natroy and Derrick were only interested in getting home and took a rain-check on dinner. I pulled onto University Parkway and turned left, heading directly into the median. "Watch it!" said Bill tapping my arm. I corrected my aim and saw Jeff's white truck in the rearview.

After following directions from the GPS's sing-song voice for an hour, I looked up and passed a sign welcoming us to Virginia. My cell rang. "Where on earth you taking us?" asked Jeff. I'd meticulously followed the instructions so I had no idea what to answer.

"They're taking us back on 87," said Bill. "We'll run into it in a few miles and drop back down." The alternate route home added another half hour to the trip. I treated Jeff and Bill to a late dinner and they agreed to pick up leaflets at the hall for distribution, starting Sunday night.

I sat in my hotel room the next morning reviewing the affidavits. All of the witnesses had done a good job and there were no significant omissions. It appeared the agents planned to ask every witness about their understanding of plant rules violated by the petitioners, and the enforcement history for the general workforce.

I opened the Charge Against Labor Organization or Its Agents attached to Neil's email. It alleged that during October, the union had "watched employees in an effort to intimidate them against engaging in protected concerted activities," and that Darnell had attempted to get Daphne fired in retaliation. Daphne Little was listed as the "party filing charge" but it was obviously an attorney's work.

The rights of American workers to engage in collective activity are defined by Section 7 of the National Labor Relations Act. The Board summarizes this entitlement as follows:

> You have the right to decide for yourself, without our interference or help, whether to support the Union, whether to support a petition to remove the Union as your bargaining representative, or not to support any of these activities.

Section 8 describes violations of these rights by employers and unions, known as *unfair labor practices*. This is a double-edged sword. Charges can be filed against a union for interfering with the rights of employees who oppose it. The Act doesn't preclude free speech unless underscored by coercion.

There was also an email from Jeff with photos attached: a new volley of postings on the employer's TV monitors, extolling the democratic virtues of the election now held in abeyance, and promising the company would champion employee rights. I sent the collection to Neil and followed up with a call. We ended up focusing on the previous week's message, characterizing the election as a choice between:

Work together directly to resolve concerns by speaking for yourself
Or
Continue to have the union to make decisions for you

I asked if the agent felt this crossed the line, referencing how management defined choice. It clearly misrepresented the union's role in collective bargaining. We don't tell people what to do. Contracts are ratified and workers elect their representatives who sit at the table.

"I agree it's a misrepresentation," said Neil. "I'll run it by my superiors but right now I don't see it involving any threats or promises. It's not against the law to lie."

The bright lights of Eden's humble shopping district faded into the winding two-lane darkness of Hwy. 158 as I drove home that evening. After two weeks in the field, I realized that I'd neglected to touch base with the union's Southern Regional Director Harris Raynor. Friday evening was usually a good time to reach him in our Atlanta office.

Regional directors tend to become overwhelmed with responsibility and constant travel. Focusing by necessity upon the organization's infrastructure and budget, they often lose touch with the humanity and compassion that originally drew them into the labor movement. But Harris is an exception. He genuinely cares about the workers and his staff.

"We've got more evidence of direct solicitation by management than I've ever run into," I told him. "And the damnedest thing is most of it comes from nonmembers. The big job is gonna be getting them to testify. Did you ever hear of this guy Fredrick Englehart?"

"No, he's new to me. I've been asking around and no one's heard of him. I never even heard of Walter|Haverfield. Who the hell are these people?"

Chapter 3. Plant Tour

I shared the details about Fredrick's background, posted on the firm's website.

"I don't understand why they didn't just use the labor lawyer they already had," said Harris. "He's with Jackson|Lewis. They're not exactly friends of labor." He speculated that his long-standing relationship with attorney Ed Cheroff had motivated him to refuse the assignment. They'd met for negotiations at another plant earlier that week but the lawyer was unresponsive when asked about Mohawk.

"Have you stayed abreast of what's been happening with the Board in Washington?" asked Harris.

The Board is an acronym with two meanings. It can either refer to the NLRB's national staff of field agents and attorneys, or to the five-member panel appointed by the president to govern the agency for staggered five-year terms. I admitted to Harris that during the intervening years I'd lost touch.

"Three of Obama's appointees are gone," he said. "They've been replaced with corporate labor lawyers and other conservatives. It's the most unfriendly Board we've ever had to deal with."

CHAPTER 4

Labor Board Investigation

There's no facet of American society more misunderstood than unions. Millions of educated people harbor passionate opinions about a world they've never known. Many assume unions are businesses profiting from the collection of dues. In reality, the federal government classifies unions as nonprofit organizations. Union dues simply provide operating expenses: offices, lawyers, staff, travel, equipment, etc. It would be impossible to effectively represent employees of well-funded corporations without similar resources.

I spent twenty years doing blue collar work, in both union and nonunion facilities, before being hired as union staff. I experienced firsthand the arbitrary and capricious manner with which workers are treated by employers free of accountability. One carries a smoldering rage deep within that slowly increases over the years.

The most significant improvement unions offer workers is *dignity and respect* in the workplace. Every union contract embodies the *Just Cause Doctrine*, binding management to strict due process in matters of discipline and discharge. Under just cause, an employee is deemed innocent of infractions unless proven guilty, and discipline is overturned when punishment outweighs the offense or rules weren't equally enforced. Workers believing their rights have been violated are represented in a grievance procedure culminating in binding arbitration.

Only in union facilities does democracy penetrate the plant gate onto the shop floor. The true value of just cause extends well beyond remedied injustices. It means that countless abuses of authority never occur, because management is aware of the consequences. An employee who comes to work and does their job need not fear losing favor with a supervisor or being bullied.

Seniority language governs job vacancies and layoffs, eliminating the inevitable favoritism that occurs in other locations, thereby providing a level of job security to tenured employees. Some nonunion companies target senior employees during workforce reductions, in favor of younger workers with lower wages and less likelihood of on-the-job injuries.

While a given round of wage negotiations is unlikely to yield life-changing results, over the years, ongoing collective bargaining significantly raises the standard of living. Weave Room employees at the Karastan plant averaged over $21 per hour in 2017.

The days leading up to the holidays were spent trying to complete my process of witness investigation, strategizing with the committee and communicating with Neil. We were under a lot of pressure. Neil informed me his office planned to render its decision by December 15 and had to allow a period for management's response to our evidence.

On Monday I asked Neil if it was time to file an *amended charge*. Our investigation had uncovered new allegations, including direct solicitation by additional members of management. The agent suggested submitting it fairly soon but asked that I refrain from referencing management by name.

I expressed surprise at what seemed an unusual request. Agents had always appreciated the specificity and added detail. Neil told me this wasn't the Region's current policy. He felt it best to avoid giving management a premature heads-up and additional time to conjure a defense.

"Should I also file an amended offer of proof?" I asked. "Some of the initial witnesses on my list didn't pan out, but some a whole lot better are willing to come forward."

"That won't be necessary. There's no need to file a second request to block a petition that's already in abeyance."

The following morning I received an amended charge filed on behalf of Daphne that added:

> Within the past six months, the Union has made coercive statements, through leaflets distributed to employees, in an effort to intimidate them against engaging in protected concerted activities.

I asked Neil for the specific leaflet statements in question and learned there was only one, from the first leaflet: "their *little pets* will be well taken care of." The agent explained the opposition was alleging we were threatening anti-union employees with hostile retaliation.

"Who do they think I am? Tony Soprano?" I asked with exasperation. "I was referring to their possible compensation by management."

Neil said he tended to agree, having read the statement in context, but all allegations had to be investigated and responded to.

Part One—The Campaign

The committee was up in arms about the charges against us when we met that afternoon, especially Darnell, who'd been cited by name.

"I don't even know what they're talking about, us watching Daphne. And saying I tried to get her fired! All I told management and a few workers was that the company had to start enforcing its rules the same for everyone. I got taught in a workshop that under the contract, they have to do that. They got no business lying about the union and slandering my good name!"

I put up my hand to stop a tirade that might have gone on for fifteen minutes. "You're reacting exactly the way Fredrick wants. Don't let this get under your skin and distract you from building our case against them. This is all in the game. I've had charges filed against me in other decert campaigns. It's like we're accusing them of bank robbery and they're accusing us of spitting on the sidewalk."

Bill asked what would happen if the Board ruled in favor of both cases and decided both sides were in violation. I assured him it wouldn't affect the Board's decision to dismiss an illegally obtained petition.

I turned back to Darnell and asked if he'd brought a copy of the plant rules. The mill chair handed me a heavily crinkled and smudged piece of paper. I requested a few minutes for review.

In the section labeled *GROUP D—WRITTEN WARNING* two offenses caught my attention:

20. Going from the department in which the employee works to another department without permission.

23. Solicitation by employees which in any way interferes with the work of employees.

I read these aloud. "Now all we got to do is prove management knew, in a way the Board will accept."

I interviewed Thomas Meadors, Darnell's brother. He might have been dismissed as uneducated by office professionals, but I sensed his inherent intelligence and ability to stay on point without becoming emotional, and engaged it.

Thomas was a maintenance worker in Weaving. He'd been on break in the canteen during mid–October when Daphne entered. She left upon catching sight of the vice mill chair. It wasn't her scheduled break time. A few minutes later, Thomas received a call on his two-way radio from supervisor Ryan Lewis, with whom he'd always been friendly. Ryan whispered, "There's something in Mending you need to see."

Thomas finished eating and went to the oil room, to begin filling oil containers necessary to service weavers. He chose this as his next duty because the raised location offered a wide-angle view of Mending. He observed Daphne and Robin going table to table with a clipboard for approximately half an hour.

Jeff walked up to me as we were locking up for the evening. "You know when we, the committee, all gets together, you should include Thomas. He's the vice mill chair."

"I'm sorry. I've just been going with the three Anthony designated to me as the leaders. Tell Thomas I apologize and he'll be there in the future."

On Wednesday morning, I received a call from an NLRB extension. The caller introduced herself as Shannon Mears, supervising attorney on the CA and RD cases. She had a couple of questions. Her name sounded familiar and I asked if we'd ever worked together.

"Yes, on Kmart. I read the article about you in Bitter Southerner. Very cool."

The union had caught a good break: the ranking supervisor knew me from the old days. We'd worked closely on a major case, creating a conduit for my credibility to flow into this one.

I typed the union's *First Amended Charge*, containing eleven allegations, many of which referenced multiple counts. The scope of management's direct solicitation was expanded, but with names omitted per Neil's request.

That evening, a young man of stocky build with long hair neatly tied back in a ponytail entered the hall. Taina motioned him to the tables where I sat with the committee. "I'm Kevin," he said shaking my hand. "Jeff said you wanted to talk to me."

He didn't require much convincing and began his story. Kevin had been employed by Mohawk for only two years but had always been a union member. He worked in Aviation Beaming with several other employees in an isolated part of the plant. One Friday evening in October, a couple of them stayed late to finish a job. Once it was completed, Kevin visited Margie's office to inform her. He encountered Margie's assistant Carolyn sitting behind a desk, who asked if anyone had talked to Kevin about the union. When told no she said they'd send someone to his department on Monday morning.

"Sure enough, Monday around 7 or 7:30 a.m., there comes Daphne and this woman named Mia Linares. Now, we work down a long flight of stairs in the basement. Hardly anyone comes to see us. I know they weren't on any break right after their shift just started. Daphne run her mouth for about ten minutes and left."

I told him we could definitely use this material and changed subjects. Kevin lived with a woman named Brenda who had friendships with some of the anti's. It was my understanding they confided in her and had shared the details of what actually occurred during the Garner trip.

Kevin became reticent. "That's true, but I've already talked to her and she don't want nothing to do with any of this. I'll try again."

I asked if he could think of anything else.

"Well, I don't know if this is important or not, but a few weeks ago, I was told by my bossman to go to the office. Ray, that Mexican guy from HR, was in there. He told me they was taking pictures for the company website and wanted to take mine. Then he asks, 'Have you heard about the petition with the union?'

"I told him, 'I've worked in nonunion plants and the company treats you like dirt.'"

"He says, 'Mohawk's not like that. It has 30,000 employees and couldn't have that many if it didn't treat them nice. This is the only plant with a union, and it would be better off without one.'"

I exclaimed this was exactly the type of evidence we were looking for. It was the second time we'd implicated Ray and I sought more information about him, including his last name. But Kevin had little to offer. He said that Ray had arrived at the plant several days after Leslie and was always out on the floor talking to workers.

"Would you be willing to come with me to Winston?"

"Just tell me when."

CHAPTER 5

The Three Girls

I slept for ten hours on Thanksgiving eve, ate breakfast in my office, resumed editing wildlife photos from the previous summer, and stumbled into the kitchen around 1:00. Patricia was busy at the oven preparing our turkey. She looked good in her new haircut: straight black hair with a few slender grey streaks, hanging just above her shoulders. Her oval face was a bit creased from a difficult journey, but her eyes still sparkled and she maintained a girlish figure. No one ever guessed her age.

I hugged her from behind and spoke as she continued stuffing the bird. "I've spent my whole life taking care of other people, since my days on the street keeping the other kids alive. But no one's ever given me a damn thing. I've had to fight and scrape for everything I've got. But you've been there for me and had my back when I was the one who needed a friend. I appreciate your sticking by me."

On Monday morning, I followed up with Neil to see if he'd made arrangements to take affidavits in Eden from our four most crucial witnesses on Wednesday.

"I haven't heard back from my supervisor," he said. "I'll ask again but can't make any guarantees."

That wasn't good enough for me. The case wasn't going to rise or fall based on bureaucracy and a young agent's inability to understand textile workers. I called Shannon and began explaining the urgency of my request. She cut me off halfway through the second sentence.

"You got it."

I requested both agents, explaining the three menders didn't get off work until 4 p.m. and wouldn't stick around all night. Shannon told me it wouldn't be a problem. As a United States attorney, she was higher in the chain of command than Neil's immediate supervisor.

Bill frequently called to discuss the case and did so on Tuesday morning from work. The platform running the length of his gigantic loom made him difficult to spot from the floor.

"About them three girls…. Annie told me today that she and the others have thought about this over the holidays, and they don't want no part of it."

"They're the heart and soul of our whole case. They're the glue that holds all the other witnesses together and makes them credible."

"I know that, but what the hell am I supposed to do? We can't drag them in front of an agent if they don't want to come."

I told him about my discussion with Shannon. Both agents would be at the union hall on Wednesday and we'd look like idiots if the women didn't show up. I suggested he talk with Annie again, explaining we'd set things up as she requested, and reiterating the importance of her testimony, supported by her two co-workers. I cautioned him to be convincing, but not to push so hard that he pushed them away.

The committee joined me at the hall that afternoon. I apologized to Thomas for leaving him out during strategy meetings.

"No problem," he calmly answered.

"Any change with the girls?" I asked Bill. "Is Troy still a go?"

"I got with all three during my break. They said they'd think about it some more. Best I could do without twisting their arm. Troy will be here right after he gets off."

I informed Bill that Neil wanted to take a supplemental affidavit from him about enforcement of plant rules, so his attendance would also be required. We reviewed potential witnesses not yet interviewed but the committee was eager to discuss our recent trip to Winston-Salem.

"Let me tell you something about when you sit down in front of a federal agent, and raise your hand to take an oath," said Bill. "It's a bit intimidating. Any thought you may have had about stretching the truth goes right out the door. Neil keeps asking you the same questions over and over, bringing them up when you least expect, to see if he can trip you up in a lie."

I told the men it was clear from reading affidavits that Neil was a good investigator and took his job seriously. I noted that Board agents were represented by a government employees union. Most of them who'd been around for awhile knew the score about what really happened in situations like ours. Unfortunately, that didn't override their job requirement to remain neutral and comply with rules and procedures before they could side with us. And how those rules were interpreted depended on who was in the White House.

Jeff interjected that Natroy Reese was very upset about how late we'd returned from Winston-Salem. She'd confronted him in the plant, complaining that her husband thought she'd been out playing around and threatened to leave her. I could only ask him to explain that no one had been more surprised than me about how long it had taken.

I called Bill from my hotel room on Wednesday morning. "I spoke with all three girls as they were coming in at the gate," he said. "Right now they're saying they'll be there at 4:00, but I can't be sure if they'll change their minds again when it's time. If Annie comes, they'll all come."

I touched base with Neil to let him know I expected all of our witnesses. I could tell he was a bit pissed about my having gone over his head, but he was a professional and would get over it.

Neil and Brent drove up the incline to the union hall parking lot at 2:45. They entered the glass doors, pulling large briefcases on wheels. There were two vacant rooms at their disposal. Anthony was traveling and his spacious office was situated at the front end of the building with a large conference table in the center. Adjacent to my work area in the rear was a small office, once belonging to a recently deceased business agent. It hadn't been cleaned in months and the empty space contained only a dilapidated desk.

"Who wants the luxury accommodations?" I asked. Though the lead agent, Neil took the smaller room. Bill and Troy arrived a few minutes after 3:00 and were both done within an hour.

I sat in my usual spot at the center table within the horseshoe formation, and Bill took his seat along the left wing. We were both silently watching the clock. I opened my laptop and got online to distract myself but it didn't work. The large clock hanging between us and the door read 4:04. The minutes slowly dragged by. *Steady as she goes*, I told myself. *Don't think.*

At 4:16 Annie entered through the glass doors. She seemed in good spirits as I walked across the floor to greet her. "I don't like the way Margie tried to do me and the others," she told me. A few minutes later she was joined by Elma and Lisa. It was nearly 8:00 before the witnesses were homebound, all of them declining a late dinner.

Neil informed me he'd be sending the four witnesses copies of their signed affidavit in the mail. Board agents travel with a portable printer so I asked why he hadn't just used his.

"I wanted to make sure you didn't get a copy of these affidavits," he answered.

"Why? What makes them different from the last set?"

"Let's just say they cover some very sensitive material and I don't think it's appropriate for you to see them at this time."

"Can you at least tell me, off the record and without going into detail, if their statements were roughly consistent with the notes I provided?"

"No. I'd rather not discuss their testimony yet."

I'd never had an agent make affidavits unavailable from consenting witnesses or refuse to engage in candid assessments. I was tired and hungry but swallowed my frustration. This was not an argument to be won and I couldn't afford to alienate these guys.

We cordially shook hands and I asked Bill to remain behind. I instructed him to have Troy and *the three girls* give him their affidavits when they arrived in the mail. He could have Taina make copies and return the originals. I wouldn't be able to file briefs in support of our case without them.

"Let's get the fuck out of here and eat at Ruby Tuesday," I suggested.

I arrived at the hall the next morning to transport my next group of witnesses to Winston. Management was responding to more union leave requests in a month than they were accustomed to receiving in a year. Some of them involved people who didn't hold office and a few weren't even members. It appeared I'd struck the right balance interpreting *reasonable requests for union leave* per the contract. The company had to be aware these individuals were witnesses. But I was providing ample notice and only requesting four people for half a shift. There was one thing management feared even more than facilitating my case: providing grounds for a second amended charge alleging interference with a government investigation.

Leila and Jeanette rode with me, followed by Thomas and Lonnie. An hour later I announced myself through the intercom beside the locked entrance of the NLRB suite. "Hell of a security system they got here," I told the group. "I give a name and union affiliation, and they let us in. I could just as easily be another Timothy McVeigh."

Neil met us on the other side. He informed me the hearing room was occupied and we'd have to wait in the lobby. A day confined to this tiny vestibule with several uncomfortable chairs and no desk was my worst Labor Board nightmare. I followed Neil to his office to provide an update regarding our investigation:

We'd identified two Human Resource executives who started camping out at the plant several weeks before the decert window opened. One of them was a director named Leslie Taylor, who normally divided her time between numerous facilities under her jurisdiction. Our people seldom remembered seeing her at the plant prior to the decertification effort. But since October she'd been observed in production areas almost daily, sometimes holding lengthy meetings with anti-union leaders. A few days after arriving, she was joined by another corporate executive, Ray Santos. He spent most of his time on the floor talking with workers. We thus far had two witnesses who could document his direct solicitation, including Jeanette Woods, who was present today.

I stared at Neil's expressionless face while summarizing my activities. "If you don't mind my asking, have you ever worked a decert case before?"

"No, this is my first. I've mainly worked charges and objections stemming from campaigns to organize new units."

I told him in my experience, there were two primary types of company supported decertifications. In one scenario, a corporation that has a good relationship with the union at a national level agrees to recognize us at a new facility without an election, if we can sign fifty percent of the workforce. Within a few months a contract is negotiated and the executives move on. Local management feels like the union got shoved down their throats and conspires to get rid of it when the first window opens.

But within an established local like this one, a decertification almost always originates at the corporate office. It tends to be sponsored either by the Human Resources or production division, with the other kept somewhat in the dark, for plausible deniability. I stated the present case had all the earmarks of an HR driven campaign.

"We'll look at all the evidence," said Neil.

We returned to the lobby and the guys followed him to the offices inside. I took a seat on a small coffee table to spare my back, facing the two women who appeared comfortable in their soft chairs. They were good company and the time passed more quickly than imagined.

We got out by 7:00 and everyone was down for dinner at Ruby Tuesday. I collected affidavits in the parking lot. Leila took the front passenger seat and we pulled out onto University Drive. She was outgoing and curious about me. "It must have taken a lot of schooling to learn what you do. Where did you go to college?"

"I didn't. Only thing I got is a Ph.D. from the School of Hard Knocks. This life ain't about being book smart. It's about knowing when to zig and when to zag without hesitating. You react and think about it afterward. College boys who aren't wired that way don't last long."

"But what led you into this. When did you first realize you had this ... calling?"

"It goes all the way back to when I was a kid on the streets of New York. I ended up being the one who looked out for the others. Let me tell you a story."

At twenty-one, I became manager of a cheap hotel populated by dope fiends, prostitutes both male and female, and just some regular folks down on their luck. There was a young man named Greg who'd just been paroled after eight years in prison ... a heroin addict in the methadone program. One afternoon he became involved in an altercation with the manager of a nearby supermarket, and the police were called. Greg made a hasty retreat because he'd been paroled in New Jersey and was in violation for being out of state.

A few minutes later the police come tearing through the building, but Greg had found refuge in the room of a biker named Shawn. The police finally left and law enforcement from three agencies took up positions surrounding the hotel. The massive tattooed biker brought Greg to my office; shaking and white as a sheet. I looked at them and said, "I've got an idea."

A lot of old buildings in New York have airshafts. They provide every room with the legally required window, but open only to a narrow brick enclosure with a huge steam pipe in the middle. I led them to the airshaft on the first floor and pointed to a window in a building caddy-corner from us. My girlfriend Soozie had become friends with two drag queens who lived in that apartment.

I told them with some rope, we could lash Greg to the steam pipe and he could shimmy around to the window. Meanwhile, Soozie could go there and notify her friends to expect company. Shawn went searching but all he could find were battery cables. The old rusty pipe was several feet around, but we tied Greg on as best we could. If the cable came undone, he'd fall several dozen feet to the rat infested basement.

I'd never seen anyone so terrified as Greg, while he gingerly inched his way around. But he made it through the window. Per the plan, Soozie and Greg stood behind the building's door, facing a street perpendicular to ours. They put their arms around each other like lovers waiting for a bus. As soon as one showed up, Greg hopped on and went to live with a friend of mine in the Bronx.

"I just do this shit because I can," I told Leila.

The following morning, I asked Neil what my deadline would be to file a brief.

"It's certainly your right to file a brief," he replied, "but it's not necessary. We're capable of examining all the evidence and making a determination."

"I always file a brief to get the union's theory of the case on record."

Neil gave me a deadline of less than a week. The group of agents and attorneys involved with the charges were still planning to make a decision before people started going on vacation. NLRB regions evaluate progress on a monthly basis and they were intent on having closure of this case credited to December.

I'd won numerous cases based on briefs, connecting the dots within complex evidentiary arrays in ways that didn't occur to the agents. I lived and breathed my investigations from the ground up and no one understood them better than me. This was the first time anyone at the Board had been anything other than appreciative of the extra effort.

CHAPTER 6

The Union Busting Lawyer

I spent the weekend typing my brief while Patricia braved the cold to prepare flower beds for spring. Ordinarily, I'd have waited until receiving all the affidavits, but it was our bad luck the holidays would trim two weeks off the normal investigation period. I resented not being given a chance to review the four critical statements taken at the union hall. The only option was to work from my notes with the assumption they accurately foreshadowed subsequent affidavits.

I presented the detailed chronology of events beginning in late September, tying each fact to specific witnesses and providing legal foundation for our interpretation. Toward the end I argued:

> Management's prevailing participation in soliciting signatures on the petition, the free plant access granted to its bargaining unit agents, meetings between Human Resource management and anti-union leaders held in work areas, and management's public statements, sent a clear and chilling message to employees that management not only encouraged, but expected their support in decertifying the union. Management dramatically exercised its leverage as the provider of livelihoods, in coercing employees to abdicate their Section 7 Rights.
>
> The specter of management at the helm creates the impression that success of the decertification is likely. This leads some employees to fear that withholding support will compromise their job security once the union is gone.

Bill called on Monday. "Meet me at the hall after work. I got affidavits from the girls. Troy forgot to bring his but said he would."

Several hours later I sat at my table studying twenty-six pages of detailed testimony. Neil had done an extraordinary job of probing for and eliciting details that filled in the blanks and brought each account to life. The women had kept their wits about them and their stories straight. I was relieved that the solid foundation we'd hoped for in our case was now cemented in place.

"This is one of the most outstanding pieces of organizing I've ever seen," I told Bill. "We'd have none of this if it weren't for you."

Chapter 6. *The Union Busting Lawyer*

I checked email the next morning at my hotel room desk and found a message from the office of Walter|Haverfield containing two attachments: **Request for Review of Decision to Block Petition 10-Rd-209088** and a supporting brief, filed directly with the NLRB in Washington.

Fredrick presented detailed arguments in an attempt to circumvent our evidence based on legal technicalities in how the union's charges had been filed, in light of the 2014 Rules and Regulations. He asked the now-conservative heads of the NLRB to overturn Region 10's decision to block the election pending investigation. His tedious legal diatribe cited the Board's Section 103.20 rule and argued:

- The union's amended charge "differed materially" from the original.
- Because of these differences, a new offer of proof should have been filed with the second charge.
- The names of Margie Clemmons and Elise Griffin were "conspicuously omitted" from the amended charge. "Instead the charge repeats the allegations that the Union specifically attributed to these two but now claims these specific acts were committed by unnamed 'members of management.'"
- The allegations in the original charge were therefore not credible and "forces the inference" that the more vague amended charge was simply an attempt to "delay processing of the petition."

I called Ira while driving toward the hall to gather my next group of witnesses for the trip to Winston. I explained to our attorney that Fredrick's entire argument was based on what Neil told me to do when filing the amended charge. We'd actually implicated additional members of management, but Neil had instructed me not to include names and that a second offer of proof wasn't necessary. While our new charge had far more substance than the original, Fredrick had done a very slick job of making it look otherwise.

"I assume you're going to file an opposing brief," I told him.

"No, I'm not. This guy's an idiot and I'm not going to respond to his bullshit."

"I've never seen a company lawyer appeal to the Board in Washington until after losing a trial at the Regional level. He's obviously playing to their more conservative make-up. I'm worried about this."

"Well, I'm not. He's an idiot. I respect what you're doing here but please don't tell me how to do my job."

"You're right this guy's an idiot. The problem is the people in his audience are also idiots. They know nothing of our case other than what Fred's told them. I don't want us fighting the uphill battle of appealing a bad decision and lost election. We need to go on record now."

"Look, I've made my decision."

The discussion was finished in the parking lot as workers waited inside. I swallowed my frustration and entered the hall to greet them. My most significant witness was Kevin, who'd been solicited by Ray Santos in his office. Two others would further document petitioners enjoying free rein within the plant, but without being able to place management on the scene. Shortly after, we were barreling through the GPS network of back roads and side streets heading toward Winston-Salem. I nearly overshot several abrupt turns but instinctively cut the wheel hard with one hand to keep us on-track. "Speed limits were made to be broken," I explained to my passengers.

During our initial meeting, I asked Neil what he thought of Fredrick's brief. To my astonishment, he hadn't been copied and I promised to forward it.

That evening I relaxed with witnesses over dinner. I asked Kevin if he'd learned anything new from his girlfriend or made any progress in getting her to testify. Following a moment of hesitation, he disclosed that Daphne sometimes confided in Brenda, who usually just listened. A few days earlier, Daphne bragged that management had promised her promotion to safety coordinator as a reward. I told Kevin that putting this on record would take the case to a whole new level.

"How do I say this?" he responded. "Brenda's the sort of person that don't like to take sides. She hates conflict. It's just how she is. I mean, if there's an argument between me and the kids, she just stays out of it and won't get involved."

I returned to the hotel at 9 p.m. and called Harris to share my discussion with Ira. The director briefed me on recent developments at the NLRB: It was becoming common practice for employer attorneys to bypass the agency on a regional level and directly approach its leaders in Washington. The current Board members were trying to consolidate control and strip regions of their authority, providing company lawyers with a unique opportunity. They were seeking a test case to use as an excuse for the Board to reinterpret its procedures, and possibly even rewrite the law.

"They hate us up there," he said. "We try to stay as far away from them as possible."

"All the more reason we need to respond," I told him. "I don't want them only viewing our case through Fredrick's eyes and overriding the Region."

Harris promised to seek a second opinion from another union lawyer and get back with me.

Ira called the next day as I drove toward the hall. "I'll be sending you a draft of my brief to review tomorrow."

"Are we going to argue that the procedures used in filing the amended charge were based on Neil's instructions? How can the union be faulted for following the Region's directive?"

"No. I'm going to argue that Fredrick had his head up his ass when he interpreted the Board's regulations and back it up with some good case law. I've got two things to say to you.... One, you're doing a really great job. Two, I'm really pissed off at you."

There were no witnesses to interview that afternoon, so it seemed like a good time to regroup with the committee and explore new leads. We took our usual seats. I sat in the middle of the center table in the horseshoe formation, with Jeff one seat over to my right. Bill took the corner seat nearest me on the left wing, with Thomas on the far end. Darnell sat by himself on the right wing.

Bill asked how our case was looking. I responded it was too early for Neil to give me an off-the-record assessment, but I felt we were doing a good job proving management solicitation. I wasn't as confident about our ability to prove the anti's had been *allowed* free run of the plant. We still hadn't met the Board's standard of documenting that management witnessed the activity.

"So what happens if the company's found guilty?" asked Darnell. "Will they have to pay a fine? Will anyone go to jail?"

"You're not gonna want to hear this, but you need to."

The only penalty the company faced was being ordered to post notices throughout the plant, promising to never again repeat each of its violations. The petition would be permanently dismissed. In the process the company would suffer negative publicity and most important, the union would survive. But that was it.

I told the mill chair it didn't frustrate him half as much as me, because I'd spent a career dealing with this. It was as if someone got caught robbing a bank, and the only penalty was to return the money and post a notice on his door saying he'd never do it again. What would be the incentive to not take another shot in six months, or for someone else to fear robbing a bank?

Mohawk was engaged in a fraudulent conspiracy to deprive American workers of their rights. But this is the only area of law where people get busted for something this serious and don't go to jail. It's the only area of law where attorneys can participate in the conspiracy, suborn perjury to cover it up, and not get disbarred. However, these were the cards we'd been dealt, and our only choice was play them to win.

"Talk in the plant is that Daphne's been going about with her head down, acting like she's really upset," said Darnell. "She told a couple of folks that she wishes she'd never gotten into all this and feels like she's become the most hated person in the mill."

"Maybe she's starting to wake up and realize that management has been playing her. I'm sure they told her it would be 1–2–3 get rid of the union and become someone important. They didn't bother to mention the type of fight this sort of thing often turns into."

I decided to ease off on my rhetoric against the anti's in our leaflets. If we played it slow and smart, perhaps Daphne could be turned.

The committee was never in a rush to disperse and we sat around fraternizing. Bill revealed a bit more about his biker affiliation and said in truth they weren't actually one-percenters. Most had jobs and one man was a union member at a Goodyear plant just across the Virginia line. But they did party with Hells Angels and Outlaws, frequently attending the same bike rallies on weekends. Someone would notify the Hells Angels out of respect and they would respond, "Sure, y'all come on down and party."

"There's folks ask me if I'm scared riding a motorcycle for hundreds of miles down the interstate, that I might wipe out one of these days. To be honest, you'd be surprised how many of our brothers we've buried. But I tell them no, I ain't afraid. If my time comes, that's just how it is."

"I understand where you're coming from," I said. "I've never been afraid to live and I'm not afraid to die. The one thing I don't want is to get stuck somewhere in between. I'd rather get my brains blown out in the field than die lying in a hospital bed with tubes up my nose."

That evening, my inbox contained two new documents by Fredrick: a motion and supporting brief for *RECONSIDERATION OF DECISION TO BLOCK PETITION*, filed directly with the NLRB's Region 10 in Atlanta. It was a second bite at the same apple. The arguments were similar to his previous brief, but this time he specifically stated that, because our amended charge had not "been accompanied by a simultaneously filed offer of proof," all of our existing evidence was moot on its face for purposes of blocking the election. I notified Ira and Harris.

There was also a letter from Neil stating it was time for him to take evidence regarding the charges against the union and requesting my position statement.

The next morning I transported two women to Winston-Salem, bringing our witness total to seventeen. They would add to our wealth of testimony regarding anti-union activity, this time in Yarn Prep and Finishing. Neil once again allowed me to set up in the hearing room and provided the day's internet password.

"Given Fredrick's briefs and the current make-up of the Board, do you think it would make sense for me to file an amended offer of proof?" I asked.

"I'm not sure. Let me call the Regional Director and ask for guidance." An hour later he walked into the hearing room and said that his director believed it would be prudent. At least I'd have something to do that afternoon. I typed an *offer of proof* containing a detailed summary of evidence already on record in our affidavits.

I ate my sandwich and prepared a leaflet announcing shift meetings on the following Tuesday and Thursday. It summed up the recent activity:

LAST MINUTE DIRTY TRICKS

This week, Mohawk's **union busting lawyer** filed a battery of motions and briefs with the NLRB, trying to use legal technicalities to overturn the *truth* we have presented. What else can they do? Mohawk *can't argue the truth*, because it's not on their side.

Imagine how much money Mohawk is paying this lawyer to play their dirty games! It makes it clear how much Mohawk wants to get rid of the union.

Bill called the next day to discuss a couple of possible leads. I asked him to pick up the leaflets at the hall when he got off work and arrange for distribution to begin on Sunday night. I then studied Ira's brief, opposing the employer's request for review of the decision to block the petition.

This was our attorney at his best. His concise and articulate analysis of Section 103.20 demonstrated that a second offer of proof was not required, especially under circumstances where there was already sufficient evidence on record to uphold the Regional Director's decision to block. Ira and I form an odd but effective partnership. We sometimes quarrel, but my street smarts balance his scholarly approach and we complement each other well in the long run. The question was to what degree his well-researched arguments would be persuasive to government officials appointed by an anti-union president.

Part One—The Campaign

That night I was interviewed on Houston's KPFT by host Ron Gonyea and discussed the witnesses who chose to have their affidavits taken at the union hall:

It wasn't a quick decision on their part. They really went through a kind of agonizing soul-searching process ... kind of a classic battle within themselves of fear versus wanting to tell the truth and do what's right.

I told them, "You know the company saw you as weak links but you have come forward and are about to prove them wrong, and you're going to feel good about that for the rest of your life." And seeing folks go through that kind of process and transformation, and finding the nerve to do it, is the most beautiful and fulfilling part of my work.

CHAPTER 7

Federal Agent's Grim Forecast

Jeff called the first shift meeting to order at 3:15 on Tuesday and I welcomed our members.

"The company says they won't cut our pay even if the union does get voted out," said a lanky black man wearing overalls and a ball cap.

"I'm glad you brought that up. It's a good place to start the meeting. So, where so you want to put your faith ... in the word of people who keep lying to you on their TV monitors, or in a signed contract that's enforceable in court? You work in the highest paid plant in the county. Who do you want to trust with that?"

I don't prepare my union hall presentations, but rather swim with the current. I asked who the members would rather trust if unjustly written-up or fired, explaining that under North Carolina law, a company can terminate workers for any reason. They all knew people who'd been railroaded out of nonunion plants just because someone didn't like them. Under a union contract they had representation and the same rights as if accused in the criminal justice system.

"We're in a war of truth against lies. Mohawk has hired this union busting lawyer named Fredrick Englehart ... you know if I were writing a book, I couldn't have come up with a better name for his character.... Anyway, he's just filed motions and briefs with the people in Washington who run the Labor Board."

I offered a user-friendly account of Fred's efforts to disqualify our evidence of management complicity based on legal technicalities and likened it to the tactics of a mafia lawyer when the truth condemns his client.

"Does anyone in their right mind want to trust these people with their livelihoods?"

Jeff remained behind after the other committee members had left. "Hey, look, there's something I need to discuss with you. Why you tell Bill about the leaflet and have him making the arrangements to give it out?

81

I thought I was supposed to be your go-to guy. I'm the president of this local."

I told him Bill had called me shortly after the leaflet was written, so I made him the point of contact and requested he pass the word. I asked Jeff if he understood the magnitude of my responsibilities. I didn't have time for unnecessary phone calls.

"Well, it's not just that. Seems like you look to him for his opinion more than others on the committee. We're all supposed to be in this together."

During unexpected confrontations, it's imperative for an organizer to maintain composure. I calmly responded that we *were* all in this together and couldn't have otherwise gotten this far. But this was a fight for our lives against a powerful and vicious company, and time was not on our side. Bill was the one committee member who'd been in the field as an organizer and had the training and instincts that go with it. Sometimes it was necessary to rely on that.

"There isn't time for me to stop and help everyone catch up. You'll learn as you go along. But right now I've got to make the right move with every step."

We shook hands and parted on good terms.

On December 12, Jeff, Bill and Darnell were scheduled to give affidavits in Winston-Salem regarding charges filed against the union. When I arrived at the hall, Taina handed me a letter addressed to litigants in the primary case, delivered to the union's email. It was signed by John D. Doyle, director of NLRB Region 10.

> This is to notify you that the petition in the above-captioned case will continue to be held in abeyance.... The Employer's Motion for Reconsideration is denied.
>
> The Union's charge encompasses conduct that could interfere with employee free choice ... affecting the showing of interest that is inherently inconsistent with the petition.

Taina ran copies for the local officers. We'd reached our second milestone but there was still a difficult journey ahead.

As we headed down side streets leading to obscure state roads I called Ira, who told me that while the company's motion had been denied by the Region, it was still under review in Washington. He characterized John Doyle as reasonable and someone the union could work with, but his decisions were subject to being overturned.

"It sounds like there's a power struggle going on within the Board at national and regional levels," I said. "If the Trump agenda prevails, the regional directors will be little more than figureheads."

"That's a fair assessment."

The affidavits took only a couple of hours and I later joined Neil for our last meeting before the holidays. As we stood in the corridor outside the hearing room, I asked what time on Friday he expected the Region to *agenda* our case. He told me the process had been postponed until "mid to late January" because the employer had requested additional response time for certain allegations.

I requested his opinion about Fredrick's tactic of appealing directly to Washington. Neil candidly responded that members of the Board had expressed interest in finding a test case to challenge the Board's *blocking charge policy*. In two recent decisions, the national panel had ruled in favor of continuing to block an election pending investigation of charges. But one contained a footnote stating that the policy would come under formal review once an appropriate case was found

"Do you think this could be that case?" I asked.

"It's possible. Before you go, I should mention this. An attorney for the National Right to Work Committee has entered an appearance on behalf of Daphne Little."

"Meaning she's going to become a separately represented party, in addition to the company and union?"

"In essence, yes."

The meeting for second shift employees was called to order at 2 p.m. the next afternoon. Jeanette Woods, sitting in her usual front row corner seat, asked what the anti's hoped to gain. North Carolina law already gave them the right to not be in the union and pay dues, so why did they care if others chose to be members?

I asked her to think about it: Most of the anti's were hired two years ago and affected during the layoff. Mohawk told them that in other plants layoffs weren't based on seniority. It was the perfect opportunity to drive a wedge between them and long-term employees. Anti's tend to be selfish people who care only about themselves. It makes them easy to manipulate.

I looked about the room. "Most of you have been here over twenty years. Daphne and the little pets are trying to strip away the seniority and job security you've spent your whole lives working for and put themselves ahead of you."

"Maybe we need to get more direct about letting them know how we feel!" exclaimed a heavyset black man wearing a leather jacket over plaid shirt, sitting in the middle. Heads nodded and there were murmurs of approval.

"Not a good idea," said Jeff. "We don't want to give Mohawk any excuses to file more charges against the union."

I complimented the local president on his observation and noted the best way to insult someone is by ignoring them. There was no law against letting Daphne know she'd lost all her friends by giving her the cold shoulder.

I reviewed our progress at the Board and offered a simplified version of the company's new legal tactics and recent defeat at a regional level. The presentation was repeated at subsequent meetings. Most textile plants shut for two weeks at year's end and I wished everyone a good holiday and well-deserved rest.

A winter's night had long ago fallen, but the committee lingered at what would be our final meeting of the current year. We were all standing at the back of the hall with our coats on.

"One day I want to be just like you," said Jeff.

I asked if he'd ever seen an old Charles Bronson movie called *The Mechanic*, and he shook his head. I offered a synopsis of the storyline: Bronson portrayed an elite Mafia hit man, skilled in tactics and every form of personal combat. He took the son of a recently assassinated mob boss under his wing.

"At some point, the young man looks up at him and says the same thing you just did to me, 'One day I want to be just like you.' Bronson answers, 'The question is, Can you pick up the tab?'"

I looked intently at Jeff. "The question is, can *you* pick up the tab?"

Jeff smiled and we all shook hands, wishing each other well over the holidays.

Long-anticipated vacations often hit me with a shock, making me feel like a saltwater fish suddenly tossed into a pond. My body and brain chemistry aren't prepared for the new environment. It felt as though six months' worth of action had been compressed into six weeks. I found myself floundering at home, back in my retirement routines but knowing better than to completely unwind.

I realized that even after thirty years of successfully presenting cases to the National Labor Relations Board, I knew little of its history and origins. Bereft of meaningful activity, I visited the NLRB's extensive website. In 1935, the National Labor Relations Act (NLRA) was signed into law by President Roosevelt. It provided employees with *Section 7 Rights*, giving them entitlement to form and join unions and compelling companies to bargain collectively, subject to enforcement by the newly formed National Labor Relations Board. Within months, the *blocking charge policy* was enacted to protect workers from hostile employers.

In 1947, the Taft-Hartley Act amended the NLRA, making unions equally subject to unfair labor practice charges. The *Right-to-Work* statute became part of the package negotiated by Congress with President Truman. It allowed states to make union membership voluntary, while requiring unions to nevertheless provide nonmembers with equal representation.

Right-to-Work is the most corrupt and hypocritical law in the industrialized world. Its sole purpose is to divide workers and undermine unions, resulting in the lower standard of living suffered by American workers, compared to European counterparts. Union resources become depleted in participating states by mandated servicing of nonmembers, and the ongoing need to invest staff time in membership drives. The labor movement strives to engage the human potential for unity and altruism. The right-to-work movement targets selfishness and greed, promoting the attitude of *why pay for something I can get for free.*

For decades, right-to-work was primarily limited to former slave states in the South. During Obama's second term, corporations and right-wing organizations began a concerted effort to spread its poison throughout Midwest legislatures. The program gained momentum under Trump until slightly more than half the states came under its influence.

While traveling abroad during the mid-'90s, I became friends with a union representative in the Netherlands. Union membership was also optional in that country, but nonmembers didn't receive representation or benefits. I could gracefully accept that arrangement in North Carolina. Union representation under right-to-work is the only service in the world to which people are entitled without contributing.

A few days into my hiatus, I decided to get the union's position statement about the CB charges out of the way. It was an informal document in which I responded to questions posed by Neil. The allegation about the leaflet was absurd to the point of inviting sarcasm:

> **Q.** State whether, in early to mid–November, the Union distributed a leaflet that said the Employer's "little pets will be taken care of." If such a leaflet was distributed, explain in detail what the Union meant in making this statement.

> **A.** This is, without exception, the most far-fetched and ridiculous allegation I have encountered during my 30 years in the field. I am the author of the leaflet.

During shift meetings preceding the leaflet in question.... I told employees that in many instances, the petitioner is offered promises of either promotion, or money, as a reward for their participation.... This was summarized in the leaflet....

Taken within context of the surrounding text in the leaflet, the intent of my remarks would be self-evident to someone with a third-grade reading level.

I have only compassion for anyone who would interpret this as a threat, and wish them success in finding a good psychotherapist to work with.

I composed music on my guitar, resumed editing wildlife photos and took walks on my property. Nature has always been my salvation and refuge. I live on a 5½ acre rectangular parcel: hilly terrain mostly covered with woodland, an old logging trail leading to a creek at the back end, and perpendicular paths I've carved out over the years. The wilderness is untamed, with coyotes, bobcats, owls, and exotic amphibians. For a kid from the streets of New York, it's like having my own state park.

Fredrick remained busy over the holidays. On December 22, he filed a second set of charges against the union, this time on behalf of the employer. The seven allegations focused primarily on exaggerated interpretations of activity and statements by committee members during October, as they tried to figure out why plant rules had been suspended for a handful of co-workers. The final allegation referenced a YouTube video made from my Houston interview:

Union official Phil Cohen, on or about December 8, appeared in a *youtube* video and made coercive, threatening statements against the petitioner.

On December 27, he filed a ***Request for Review of Second Decision to Block Petition 10-RD-2090881*** and a supporting brief, before the Board in Washington, disputing John Doyle's recent letter denying his appeal and upholding the election block.

Patricia and I sat in the living room on New Year's Eve in our lounge clothes, frantically searching the satellite menu for a movie worth watching. I'm sentimental about Christmas and Thanksgiving but have no use for New Year's. I don't drink or use drugs and despise dance music. People go to parties looking for adventure and a break from their boring routine. I'm a professional adventurer and at this point, crave only peace and beauty when not on duty.

"If most folks could see us now," I told her, "they'd think we were the two sorriest people on the planet and needed to get a life."

I surfed through a few more listings and turned back toward her. "I'm really glad you stayed sober since we got together. But you know … you've always followed the lead of whatever man was in your life. If I became a heroin addict, would you become one also?"

"I don't know," she smiled and shrugged her shoulders. "But I do know one thing. If you hadn't taken me in, I'd be out on the streets right now, doing who knows what with who."

PART TWO

The Case Unfolds

If your opponent is of choleric temper, seek to irritate him.
Pretend to be weak, that he may grow arrogant.
—Sun Tzu, *The Art of War*

CHAPTER 8

National Right
to Work Attorneys

The New Year got off to a slow start. The union's witnesses had been presented and all we could do was await management's response and the Board's analysis. I called Neil to see where things stood. Based on discussions with his supervisor, he felt the Board was leaning toward issuing complaint regarding management solicitation. He requested this unofficial position not be made public. I asked if this would be sufficient to dismiss the petition.

"That will ultimately involve a second decision making process," he said, "but in my opinion it should."

"What about *free rein*?"

"At this point we're leaning against it."

Under previous presidential administrations, I wouldn't have been overly concerned. Management solicitation is the ultimate proof of a company-supported petition. But we had entered a whole new era, where a Labor Board consisting of a Trump-appointed majority was seeking opportunities to reinterpret the law. I was staring down a long road paved with appeals, possibly resulting in a trial and then adjudication in Washington. I could envision Fredrick arguing that a couple of rogue supervisors didn't signify a company plot.

"We need to brief our free rein argument," I told Ira. We agreed upon our usual method of collaboration. I'd present the evidence supported by excerpts from affidavits, and Ira would weave citations from prior cases into our arguments.

We were failing the classic test in proving management had knowledge of free rein. None of our witnesses who'd been solicited on their jobs could place management in sufficient proximity to observe the anti-union activity. The union needed to offer a different perspective.

I reviewed all seventeen affidavits and uncovered two smoking guns that had previously escaped everyone's attention. Thomas Meadors had been alerted by his supervisor that Daphne and Robin were in the Mending Department. Why didn't the supervisor enforce the rules himself? Leila Mangold had complained about the same incident to her supervisor, who declared that he "wasn't going to put up with this." Why did solicitation in Mending then continue throughout October? We used this to underscore volumes of testimony from workers solicited on their jobs.

Ira supported our position with thirteen case citations and argued:

> Approximately six employees engaged in "open, frequent, and widespread" solicitation of signatures during working time in working areas. Supervisors must have observed this solicitation—or must have known to stay away when the solicitors showed up in departments where they did not belong.
>
> When they were soliciting in other departments, the solicitors were away from their own departments. These were relatively small departments—of no more than a dozen employees—in which supervisors usually worked on the floor. The frequent absence of two employees—Daphne Little and Mia Linares—must have been especially apparent to the Commercial Aviation supervisor, and its department head, Margie Clemmons.

I traveled to Eden on Friday to regroup with the committee and entered the union hall with my leather jacket draped over a grey sweatshirt and jeans, energized by the unmistakable feeling that this was where I was meant to be. I greeted Taina, who notified me Harris had listed the union hall for sale. The Southern Region of Workers United was progressively downsizing in response to America's dwindling industrial base. The two locals actively using the hall no longer justified paying for its upkeep. Anthony had announced his retirement later in the year, and administration of his locals would be consolidated with the Mid-South District out of the Atlanta office. I knew the funky old building, located on a hill several miles beyond the business district, would be a tough sell and hoped we'd keep it for the campaign's duration.

Once seated, I informed committee members there had been significant new developments on the legal front. I requested they permit me to review them thoroughly without interruption and before asking questions. It would allow us to disband at a reasonable hour. I rose from my seat, stepping back several feet to take in the whole group, and began updating them on Fredrick's latest brief and second set of charges against us.

"Why they keep telling these lies and dragging our names through the mud?" asked Darnell. "It ain't right."

"Please, let me go through everything on my list and we'll get back to this," I said. Darnell nodded.

I reviewed my discussion with Neil to start the New Year on a hopeful note, with the strong admonition they honor my pledge of confidentiality. I told them while the Board seemed to be leaning our way in regard to dismissing the petition, the agency didn't seem to be buying our argument about the anti's being given free run of the plant. If we ended up in court, I wanted it to be with our full case. Ira and I were working on a brief to hopefully change their minds.

"There's something going on in the plant I think…" Jeff said before I held up my hand and continued.

My biggest concern was that a lawyer from the National Right to Work Committee had entered an appearance on behalf of Daphne. I described them as an anti-union coalition in Washington made up of lawyers and businessmen, with the influence and resources to lobby Congress. They were currently sponsoring dozens of bills to strip union workers of their rights, including the very laws we were using to build our case. Their attorneys were getting involved in situations like ours across the country, looking for test cases to change the law.

"The RTW website promotes them as a 'grassroots movement' and defenders of democracy," I told them. "They're actually a front for big business with a $25 million war chest. These guys are fanatics. They're America's version of the Taliban, only they carry briefcases instead of AK 47s."

"Looks like Daphne's ego gonna get all puffed up again, now that she got her own lawyer," said Bill. "So much for being able to turn her around."

The battlefield map having been updated, I shared some of my reflections over the holidays. The Karastan workforce had a truly unique makeup for an old textile mill. The senior people are usually divided between those who support the union and those who hate it. But I hadn't sensed much animosity while walking through the plant. Some of our best witnesses were actually senior nonmembers, who obviously supported the union in their hearts or they wouldn't have come forward. Mohawk's strategy was one of divide and conquer. We needed to be pulling people together. I asked what they thought about inviting nonmembers to our next shift meetings.

Thomas thought it was an excellent idea, noting there were former members who withdrew after being offended by a committee member in the distant past. "We should give them an opportunity to see firsthand for themselves how things are different now."

The others readily agreed. I reviewed the new charges filed against us but people were tired and it was a short discussion. Jeff asked for a word in private as we adjourned.

"How come when I had something to say you raised your hand to hush me, but when Bill cut in you let him finish. I had something important that you needed to hear also."

I apologized for giving offense but noted there had been a lot of ground to cover and I needed to remain focused. Bill had been responding to what I was saying, rather than changing the subject. "We're in a war and I've got to move fast and make decisions. Sometimes I've got to risk stepping on toes, even people I consider friends."

We shook hands and locked up the building together. I appreciated that while Jeff didn't hesitate to speak his mind, he was then able to listen and let go.

I wrote a meeting announcement over the weekend. Taina was kind enough to come in on Sunday to run copies for Jeff to pick up that evening. The message ended with:

> The **union busting lawyer** tried to get our evidence thrown out on legal technicalities. He failed!! He's trying again in the New Year. He'll fail again!!
>
> We're in a fight of ***truth against lies***. The anti-union workers are nothing more than company puppets. Mohawk is pulling the strings.
>
> Management underestimated us. They thought we were weak and stupid. Mohawk is learning the hard way that we're neither.
>
> More details about what's coming next at the meetings
> *Members and nonmembers are welcome*
> **The Union is Here to Stay!**

Jeff welcomed second shift workers to the union hall on Wednesday afternoon. Turnout was somewhat lower in the New Year. The immediate crisis of a pending election had been dealt with and workers were being updated in leaflets. I filled in the blanks and discussed Fredrick's ongoing barrage in context of the Trump administration's anti-union agenda. "There's something dark and ugly sweeping across America ... but it stops here in Eden. We hold the line no matter what."

"Does this guy have nothing better to do than sit around all day typing up this nonsense?" asked one of the women who'd accompanied me to Winston.

"What you've got to remember is this guy's getting paid $400 an hour while he types and Mohawk's got money to burn."

People nodded their heads and I continued, pointing out a significant distinction that had recently occurred to me: We were at war with Mohawk, not Karastan. Incorporating this into the union's message would further unite workers and lay groundwork for future reconciliation with local management.

"This is where y'all work and earn a decent living," I told them. "Most of you are proud of the products you make." The plant had been union-ized since shortly after opening. We'd had issues with Karastan over the years but always worked things out. But the mill was now operated by a huge anti-union corporation. They were the ones responsible for hiring Fredrick.

I explained there were tactics that could "really jam up" the plant's operation, but they wouldn't be utilized. This was a shaky business in what remained of a fragile industry. We wanted Karastan to be successful. It wouldn't matter that the union survived if we no longer had a place to work. So we were going to beat them at the Board.

"But trust me on this: I'll die and burn in hell before they run this plant without a union."

It was ten minutes before the arrival of first shift and Jeff got off his phone. "Daphne's been going around the plant saying she's coming to the meeting." The seats began to fill and I kept one eye on the door.

"That's her," Jeff whispered as a young woman with shoulder length blond hair accompanied by a short, slender Hispanic man entered the hall. "He was also on the trip to Garner."

I intercepted them at the front of the hall with a certain amount of curiosity.

"You must be Daphne," I said and introduced myself.

"I know who you are and where do you come off writing those things about me in these leaflets and talking about me on YouTube?" She looked up at me, stepping closer and pointing to my first leaflet. Her histrionic tirade accelerated into high gear. "You got no business calling me names."

I felt none of the outrage one might expect, but rather a bit sorry for her as I tried to calm her down. It somewhat reminded me of fights with crazy girlfriends from my past. "We're on opposite sides of a labor dispute. I'm not going to stand here and explain my tactics to you. But it's not per-sonal. I'm here to do a job. I don't hate you. If I saw you broken down by the side of the road, I'd give you a ride."

Daphne paused for a moment but then continued venting. I cut her off this time. "I've got a meeting to run and you've got to leave."

With a look of righteous indignation she pointed to the line on my recent leaflet saying nonmembers were welcome. I responded it didn't apply to her and she wasn't going to be allowed in the meeting to gather intelligence for her lawyer.

"I don't have a lawyer."

"The hell you don't," I said firmly and she finally left, followed by her escort.

I returned to the committee and faced the membership. "Hope y'all enjoyed the show. You've got to admit one thing. She had a lot of guts coming down to the union hall like that."

I wrote Justin to schedule a plant tour the following week. This time he requested contractual justification specific to the visit and I responded:

> I periodically tour all facilities in which I represent employees, to observe working conditions, health and safety conditions, and contract compliance.

Ira forwarded a letter from Fredrick regarding the visit. The company lawyer acknowledged my contractual right to plant access, but noted the union had not "availed itself" of this right in years, and concluded by stating that Mohawk would continue to comply unless:

> the Company determines that Mr. Cohen is requesting access as part of what Mr. Cohen has referred to as "the greatest show to ever hit town."

So, you read my book, I thought. *How much did you bill for your reading pleasure?*

I spoke with Ira regarding evidence of two management violations that came to light during the recent shift meetings. It was questionable whether we could unearth sufficient evidence to support one, and if the other would be considered serious enough for inclusion in a complaint.

"Give them hell any way you can," said Ira, who'd been yanked farther out of retirement by this campaign than he'd ever imagined.

Neil suggested I file a new charge rather than amend the current one, so as not to delay processing. He remained confident there would be a determination on our main charge by month's end.

The plant visit was cancelled due to the worst blizzard to hit North Carolina in years. The factory shut for two days. Patricia and I remained trapped on our property far longer, waiting for twelve inches of snow to melt and nature to then release us from the muddy quagmire of our parking spaces. The clearing of small two-lane roads in a rural county is not a state priority.

"The Russians live like this all winter," said Patricia as we languished in our lounge clothes. "All they can do is drink vodka and have sex."

"The second option sounds like a good idea. Should we take a shower?"

That evening, I walked into her office at the opposite side of the house from mine and asked if she wanted to do a cartoon for the Mohawk campaign. Patricia looked up from her computer where she was killing time on Facebook and asked what I had in mind. I suggested a union busting attorney sitting behind his desk … similar to a cartoon we'd done at BTR in the '90s, but with remarks tailored to Mohawk. It didn't need to resemble Fredrick because no one in the plant had ever seen him, but I requested she visit his webpage to capture his ambiance.

Patricia began sketching the next morning. Her work is far more intricate than most political cartoons. She was trained in fine arts and applies it to every medium. She drew the image and text with a light blue pencil and I frequently reviewed her progress. Our intimate relationship doesn't interfere with working together as professionals. "I really like that," I told her, pointing to the attorney's face, "but over there is the exact opposite of what I wanted. Please fix it."

Once the blue line was finished, she placed a second sheet of paper over the original, turned on her light table, and carefully traced the image with a lead pencil. The basic layout was complete but could still be refined. Following my approval, the drawing was once again traced with ink and subtle details were added. The cartoon was then scanned and sent to my computer. I experimented importing and positioning the picture within a Word document, optimistically adding a victory headline on top.

The snow melted but there was still nowhere to go. I started referring to this period as the *doldrums*. Following two months of strong wind in my sails, the air was suddenly motionless. It was a peculiar situation to be running a campaign part-time. Before retirement, when a campaign slowed my attention would shift to other locals. But now I was starting to exist in an agonizing limbo. I couldn't unwind and resume writing while I remained on alert for the unexpected, which could present itself by phone or email at any moment.

I can focus my will like a laser beam into any project and sculpt it to my design, but my attention isn't easily divided. I perked up instantly when Neil or a committee member called, then drifted back into ennui.

Patricia and I aren't easy people to live with, but over time we've come to understand and tolerate each other's rough edges. But when one of us is having difficulties, the balance sometimes tips. My partner has amassed and retained more information on countless subjects than an encyclopedia. Sometimes her knowledge is fascinating, but she suffers from the compulsion to download it uninvited. When all I need is to be left alone in silence, this proclivity drives me crazy.

I was trying to prepare a quiet lunch one afternoon when she strolled into the kitchen and began chatting. "I'm trying to run a fucking campaign," I barked at her. "I don't need to hear about the history of thirteenth century Poland right now."

I ate lunch in my office, checked emails but found nothing significant, and located my best friend sitting with a lowered head at her desk. "Sorry I hurt your feelings. I'm really strung out. Want a hug?"

She rose slowly and put her arms around me. "Why have you stuck around and put up with me all these years?" I asked.

Patricia stepped back and looked me in the eye. "It's a dirty job but someone's gotta do it."

During late January, I received an emergency call from Bill. Troy Craddock, our witness who'd implicated the Human Resource manager, was on the verge of being fired for poor attendance. All the vice president could offer was that supervisors had always found Troy an excellent worker but that for several months he'd been missing work.

The Karastan plant had the most peculiar attendance policy I'd ever encountered. Most large employers give workers a certain number of *no fault* days to miss work each year. They are progressively notified along the way and discharged if the threshold is passed. Karastan employees were prohibited from missing more than 8 percent of scheduled hours within a calendar month. Each violation resulted in a *Group D* written warning. The second Group D warning within six months carried a suspension and the third resulted in discharge.

My first line of inquiry when investigating attendance cases is to ask if the employee had a chronic record of poor attendance: someone who'd successfully played the system for years until pushing the envelope a bit too far. When that's not the case, I probe for mitigating circumstance that might be upheld under just cause, or medical conditions covered by the Family and Medical Leave Act (FMLA).

The best kept secrets in America involve workers' rights mandated by state and federal law. Management is seldom forthcoming about these entitlements because they cost money and limit control. Companies post the required documents about FMLA, workers comp, sexual harassment and discrimination, but take no initiative to further educate employees. The government postings are vague and fraught with omissions. Without exception, workers only learn the full extent of their rights in a union plant.

Enacted under the Clinton administration in 1993, FMLA allows *twelve weeks* of unpaid medical leave for documented illness or injury suffered by employees or immediate family members. These absences cannot be counted against attendance policies. Much of this is unnecessary under union contracts providing *twelve months* of medical leave with job security. However, the number one best-kept secret in America is the *intermittent leave* provision of the Act.

The average person with awareness of FMLA believes it pertains to long term absences for surgery, pregnancy, etc. Intermittent leave covers ongoing conditions not requiring drastic intervention, but rather periodic doctor visits or days at home. Once certified, employees become immune to an attendance policy when citing their documented circumstances. Notice of this provision is conspicuously absent from the workplace posting. Employers despise intermittent leave above all else because of its potential for abuse.

I spoke with Troy and discovered his two-year-old twin boys had medical conditions resulting in most of his absences since October. Kyle had come down with pneumonia, requiring several days of bed care. This was mainstream FMLA and should have been certified. Brady had been born with a neck deformity, requiring physical therapy twice per month during working hours, invoking the right to intermittent leave. I felt sympathetic toward this valiant young father, struggling to take care of his two small children. But I was also concerned about losing a key witness if we went to trial.

Prior to 1993, workers in nonunion plants were at the arbitrary mercy of management when absences due to serious illness exceeded the attendance policy. Pregnant women were routinely forced to work until the very end and return sooner than appropriate after childbirth. Though employers fumed over passage of the Family and Medical Leave Act, it was a dim shadow of regulations in many European countries, requiring companies to pay workers on medical leave. The FMLA is enforced by the Department of Labor, a federal agency distinct from the NLRB.

On January 30, I pulled into Mohawk's parking lot for my rescheduled plant tour and met Jeff in the showroom upstairs. I was once again captivated by the beauty of luxury rugs hanging from the walls. I'd never been at war in a facility that produced works of art.

Jeff accompanied me to the back of the room for privacy as I further briefed him on my plant visit strategy: Over the years, I'd listened to workers expressing resentment of management figures who walked down the aisle without looking up to even say hello. I'd learned from it. The most essential ingredient of leadership is human contact and that was our primary agenda. I asked Jeff to lead us on a path where we could run into as many people as possible, including the half-dozen breakrooms that would provide opportunities to speak with workers, without management being able to argue interference with production.

A middle-aged man of medium build and height with short black hair entered the room. "I'm Greg Lovett, Justin's assistant. He's tied up in meetings so I'm going to be conducting the tour with you." We were soon joined by a department head I'd never heard of, because his name hadn't appeared in any of the affidavits.

Jeff led us through the several weaving areas and then into Mending and Yarn Prep, stopping off at every canteen. I shook hands and made eye contact with everyone along the way. Folks were warming up to me, understanding that federal agents were now investigating people who'd always held sway over their lives.

"That's Margie Clemmons," said Jeff pointing toward a loom platform in Aviation. I looked over my shoulder but saw only a weaver, my curiosity frustrated. Twenty minutes later Jeff pointed her out again, this time standing at the end of an aisle as we approached … an older woman with a frumpy build and short white hair barely covering her ears. I quickened my pace but she pivoted and disappeared.

Jeff and I accompanied Greg back to the front office complex to discuss Troy's situation with Elise. We were joined by Leslie Taylor. The corporate director took a keen interest in my presentation, clearly not wanting to open a new legal front in a situation unexpectedly spiraling out of her control. She maintained her composure and southern charm, smiling while taking notes and asking questions.

I reminded her that employers had an affirmative burden to inform workers when their situation invoked even the possibility of FMLA certification. The law holds management to a higher level of awareness than hourly employees. FMLA becomes retroactive when even a floor supervisor knew the reason for absence but remained silent. Elise agreed to provide Troy with the necessary forms for his doctor to fill out.

The next morning, Neil informed me the Board's decision had been postponed until early February, claiming his supervisor pointed out several overlooked details in the affidavits that needed to be investigated.

Ira also called with unexpected news. He and his girlfriend had long-standing reservations to visit the Far East, and they would soon be leaving the country for six weeks. An Atlanta attorney named Mike Schoenfeld would be taking over the case, though Ira expected to remain involved in writing briefs upon his return. Mike was outside counsel with a firm representing unions.

This development was somewhat unnerving. I'd met Mike over the phone a year before, helping him prep for an arbitration with a familiar local. He'd impressed me as bright and aggressive. But Ira and I had resolved our early differences and were now synchronizing effortlessly, with great impact. I wasn't comfortable changing horses in midstream during a deluge.

Ira prepared a twelve-page memo to Mike, providing a detailed analysis of the case. He expected Region 10 to issue its determination by February 9, finding merit to the union's charge of management solicitation, but incorrectly rejecting the *free rein* portion of our case. Ira raised concerns stemming from his assessment:

- The new conservative Board was seeking a test case to repeal its existing policy requiring automatic dismissal of petitions tainted by direct employer involvement.
- The Employer and National Right to Work Committee might request a *causation hearing*. If granted, this would place an affirmative burden on the union to prove Mohawk's violations impacted specific signatures on the petition.
- We must be prepared to meet this threat with the strongest possible case.
- The employer's appeal of the blocked election was still under review in Washington.

CHAPTER 9

Illegal Discharge

On February 2, I returned to Winston-Salem with two witnesses providing affidavits for our new charge. Darnell would offer evidence about plant closing rumors we hoped could be linked to management. A gentleman named Lewis had information about Mohawk bypassing the union and negotiating breakroom conditions directly with employees. The metallic female voice coming from my phone led us through the familiar, but still confusing journey.

"Anthony told me you used to drive taxis in New York City," said Darnell from the rear seat. "He made it sound dangerous. Were you ever frightened?"

"Every night. There's no dishonor in being afraid. The test of character is how you handle it." I offered to paint him a portrait of fear:

Most of the taxis in the 1970s were owned by large fleets, more crooked than any company I've since dealt with. Their cabs ran 24/7 through terrible driving conditions, and the law required them to buy new ones every eighteen months. But as the deadline approached, fleets would get a letter from their dealership, *apologizing* for a six month delay in delivery. Since the old cars were already paid-off, it meant six months of pure profit for the companies. For drivers, it meant going out every shift in a death-trap.

I was driving one of these old wrecks on a hot summer night in August when I picked up an elderly lady at 1 a.m., going to the worst part of Brooklyn. It took forty-five minutes to reach her neighborhood. The temperature and humidity were still brutal, but I rolled up my window as we turned off Atlantic Avenue and down side streets. She directed me to her building in a row of tenements, with a small park across the street. Groups of young men were hanging out every twenty yards.

The old woman opened her door but then sat there fumbling through her purse. Fleet cabs had no air conditioning and I was soaked in sweat like I'd been standing under a shower. My engine cut off. I turned the ignition but heard only grinding noises. I checked my rearview and the passenger was still searching for her money. I looked out the front window and heads were facing in my direction. I tried the key again ... the engine turned over then quit. Several guys started slowly moving my way. I waited a few seconds because if the carburetor flooded, I was dead. Realizing it was now-or-never, I tried again. The motor kept grinding and I stopped before killing the battery. Sweat was burning my eyes and it became difficult to see clearly.

"Let me tell you something," I confided to my current passengers. "If a person didn't have religion beforehand, they find it real quick in a situation like this. I looked deep inside myself and asked God: *Please let the car start. Just get me over the bridge back to Manhattan. I don't care if I break down after that.*"

The old lady finally handed me her fare and left. I cranked the ignition. The motor backfired and then started chugging. I put the taxi in gear, slowly pressed the gas pedal and began moving past the men approaching me. A couple of them banged on the trunk and hooted as I went by.

Every time I stopped for a light, I idled in neutral with my left foot on the brake, while gently nudging the gas pedal with the other foot so the engine wouldn't cut off. I never stopped praying. It took ten minutes to make it back to Atlantic Avenue and another fifteen to reach the bridge.

"I bet you called it quits for the night after that," said Lewis.

"No, I kept working until dawn. A man's gotta earn a living."

We were ushered into the NLRB lobby by the receptionist at 1 p.m. Neil met with me in his office for a few minutes to review the seven new allegations against the union. I asked how the company could suggest an interview on a Houston radio station *coerced and intimidated* Daphne in exercising her Section 7 rights in Eden, North Carolina. Nobody in Houston even knew who she was.

Neil couldn't resist chuckling. "I've listened to the interview and found nothing to support the employer's position. However, I will be sending you a request for evidence on the two allegations concerning statements made by committee members in October."

Once again, I was situated in my usual waiting area. It had been bad enough being confined to my property with nothing to do, but being trapped in an empty hearing room tested the limits of my sanity. I began referring to it as being *bored at the Board.*

Five days later I met with committee members to discuss the pending decision about our main case, expected by week's end. I told them that in every decert I'd ever fought, with one exception, once a complaint was issued proving management involvement, the employer entered into a settlement with the Board and put an end to hostilities. Companies are run by business people who look on a failed decert as an investment that didn't work out and move on. If that happened here, we'd need to be thinking about rebuilding a relationship with local management.

"I'm not interested in having a relationship with these people," said Darnell, "not after the way they tried to do us and slander our good names."

I counseled him that we likewise needed to think like business people. I wasn't suggesting trust, but a certain level of cooperation would be needed to resolve grievances and other issues quickly to serve our members. Our job was part knowing how to fight and part diplomacy. Professionals don't hold grudges.

"Can I change the subject for a minute without you cutting me off?" asked Jeff. I agreed and he asked what happened during the case where management didn't settle the charges.

It was *Highland Yarn Mills*. The company was represented by a union-busting firm in Spartanburg that appealed the Complaint all the way to Washington. We prevailed and it established precedent for similar cases. Our lawyers were currently citing it. But there was an interesting footnote. After a three-year fight, the corporate office sent in an executive vice president to negotiate a new contract. One evening, I asked why the company had gone through all this. It would have cost them far less to reach accommodation with the union than had been paid to their lawyers.

He responded, "Tell me about it. We paid them $600,000 ... and that was just for the first year-and-a-half. I still don't have figures for the rest."

Union-busting lawyers are like gun runners in a war. They only get paid as long as the fight continues. Their loyalty isn't to the companies they represent, but to their firm, which only cares about billable hours. I couldn't prove that was happening in Eden but it sure felt like it.

I called Neil after lunch on February 9 to find out where the decision stood and how long it would take for the formal written document.

"We're not going to agenda today," he said. "There were some schedule conflicts among the supervisors and attorneys. I expect it will happen soon."

A natural protagonist becomes stifled by an endless waiting game, like a fire deprived of oxygen. But on Sunday evening I had to shove my on-switch into high gear for an interview on Detroit's WDTK. One of the hosts worked as a management consultant and commented:

I've been brought into management meetings under pretenses they wanted to discuss Human Resource policies. And you go to the meeting and they say, "We'd like to know how to decertify this union."

I've said to them at that point, "This is an illegal conversation and that we can't have this conversation." On more than one occasion I've had some manager say to me, as well as a CEO, "Our competitor decertified a union and we want to do it also."

The next week brought little new activity but some positive news. Neil grew increasingly uncertain about the agenda timeline for our primary case but mentioned an interesting development regarding our latest charge. While reviewing documents and affidavits from the union's first set of allegations, agents had found evidence that the employer deliberately transferred Daphne to third shift for the purpose of soliciting employees who work at night. Neil said the union might consider amending this allegation into its new charges.

Taina scanned and emailed a hard copy document sent to the union office by the NLRB in Washington:

ORDER

The Employer's Requests for Review of the Regional Director's determination to hold the petition in abeyance are denied because they raise no substantial issues warranting review.

In this instance, current law had prevailed over political bias. Fredrick's sixty-one pages of motions and briefs had been to no avail, and Region 10 would maintain jurisdiction over its investigation and ultimate determination.

Darnell called a few days later to inform me Troy had been "walked out," referring to a one-day suspension received for attendance violations in January. Troy had promptly submitted his documentation and been FMLA certified for both children. I called Elise, who momentarily seemed taken aback to hear from me, but then explained the doctor hadn't commenced certification for one of the children until February 1.

I asked Troy to meet me at the union hall and bring his FMLA paperwork. We sat at the back table and like most employees with serious issues, he unleashed a barrage of emotionally laced opinions and information that was of no use to my investigation. I requested a few minutes to review his FMLA forms. The four-page document poses questions to the treating physician and provides lines for handwritten answers. The form pertaining to Brady's ongoing physical therapy appointments contained responses to key questions as follows:

Part Two—The Case Unfolds

Approximate date condition commenced: 2/1/2018
Estimated treatment schedule: 2/1/2018–8/1/2018

I refrained from bursting into a tirade of profanity, as Troy was religious. He'd presented the form to his child's doctor on February 1, who like an idiot, cited this as the starting date of treatment, even though Brady had been under his care since birth. Management was no doubt also aware of the discrepancy, but only legally required to follow the letter of what the physician had written.

I told Troy that my number one job frustration was doctors who didn't take the time to correctly fill out FMLA paperwork. Most of them had led sheltered, ivory tower lives, "daddy bought kids" who'd never done a day's real work in their lives. They understood nothing about the reality of ordinary people striving to maintain a job within the matrix of employer regulations; too obtuse to even realize if fired, their patient would lose the benefits paying for treatment.

I instructed Troy to present a clean form to his son's physician and explain the necessary corrections. We rehearsed for fifteen minutes until he had it right. I suggested mentioning his union representation and that the doctor really didn't want to make my acquaintance.

The days resumed flowing like a murky river through one week into the next. I remained in a state of boredom infused with high-alert tension, unable to either relax or make progress. On February 26, I called Mike to see if he had an opinion regarding the state of limbo into which our case had descended.

He informed me that he'd been in touch with lawyers handling cases across the country and none of the NLRB Regions had been issuing decisions. Everything appeared to be on hold. Company attorneys were privately expressing frustration that it was costing them money. "No one at the Board will tell me anything. My best guess is we're seeing some sort of work stoppage at a regional level to protest Washington's efforts to hijack their authority."

Neil professed no knowledge of a national policy to withhold decisions. He sounded sincere. Awareness of such extreme measures would probably remain confined to a higher administrative level.

The next morning I was interviewed on WNYM in New York City and discussed my strategies for dealing with hostile management under varied circumstances:

What I tell workers is that management is always taking notes on us. What you need to do is never come to work without a pad and pen. Take notes and document any suspicious or unprofessional conduct by management.

Host Joe Maniscalco asked me to profile the type of individual susceptible to management recruitment in a decertification drive:

The company chooses people who, to borrow a phrase from Milton, would rather rule in hell than serve in heaven.

Workers in Eden also needed to hear from us if the campaign was going to maintain momentum. I wrote a leaflet titled ***Fight Against Union Busters: Labor Board Update***. It began:

The National Labor Relations Board has become backlogged across the country. Countless decisions have been delayed, including ours.

This was followed by a review of our case, with Patricia's cartoon of *The Union Busting Lawyer* at the bottom. It was emailed to Taina and I arranged for committee pick-up the next day.

I was in the parking lot of a shopping mall, running errands with my

107

phone off at 2 p.m. on February 28. A voice inside that I never ignore told me to check messages. There was one from Taina sent an hour before: "I've run copies of your leaflet but something doesn't look right. There's a headline on top with a cartoon on the bottom, and a big blank space in between."

I called the hall and she read it out loud. I'd accidentally sent the earlier draft announcing a Labor Board victory, with an empty space awaiting text between the headline and cartoon. Taina had just saved me from the most embarrassing mistake of my career. The company would have had a field day with the false announcement and regained credibility. Damage control would have been an uphill battle.

I told her to throw it away and tell the committee to wait for tomorrow. I'd send the correct version when I was back at my computer.

"Thank you," I told Taina. "You really saved my ass by calling. I owe you big time."

CHAPTER 10

Cartoons

I've watched college-educated union organizers from middle class backgrounds in action. Many believe their true mission is to politically educate workers. But people who spend eight hours a day on boring, exhausting jobs feel only disdain for intellectuals who've never gotten their hands dirty. When the action slows in the real world, people don't remain engaged because of rhetoric. You have to keep them entertained.

Patricia's cartoon was a hit and I decided to expand the concept into a series. I requested a picture of Daphne walking in a park with a dog collar around her neck. The union-busting lawyer would be holding the chain and thinking *I just love walking my little pet.* Daphne's picture could be found on her Facebook page.

Fredrick filed a new charge against the union based on my radio interview the previous week:

> Union official Phil Cohen ... made coercive, threatening statements about the petitioner.... During the interview, Cohen said the following:
> I've stood in front of membership meetings and said look, this guy or gal is now in our gun sights and one way or another we are going to take them out and sometimes it takes a year, but once I make the commitment, that person ends up gone.

This guy's watched too many gangster movies, I thought, and called Neil. I began to explain how this out-of-context remark referred to my process for discrediting hostile members of management, but he cut me off.

"I've already listened to the interview and didn't find anything that merits investigation."

Neil took telephone affidavits from three witnesses regarding two of seven allegations contained in Fredrick's December charge. The agent didn't consider this testimony warranted a trip to Winston-Salem.

A few days later I drove home from a committee meeting on a cold, moonless night. The well-lit Hwy. 14 slowly darkened into the hills and curves of Hwy. 158. My reward for a day in the field was always a protein bar, held in one hand while I steered with the other. A nagging voice in back of my head kept telling me I should discuss the Daphne cartoon with Mike. My efforts to dismiss it were unsuccessful.

Most lawyers are risk-averse. I consider myself risk-savvy. I've built a career on taking calculated risks and getting away with it. I'm especially disinclined to have lawyers review my leaflets. They inevitably eviscerate them, leaving only boring statements of legal hyperbole that are of no interest to workers. I kept driving and wrestling with myself but my gut shouted at me to call.

"Don't do it," said Mike. "Leave the petitioner alone. We can't be perceived as coercing her in the exercise of her rights."

"Isn't this First Amendment protected? This would just be a visualization of what I've already been calling her in leaflets."

"It is protected but consider this: We end up in a trial. You can already see where Mohawk is going with its charges against us. They're trying to turn the tables and portray us as the ones violating people's rights. Even though the Region isn't sympathetic, the company lawyer can still bring his arguments to court. Imagine Fredrick presenting this cartoon to a judge who doesn't know us. Let's not do anything to screw up our case."

"You got it. The cartoon's out."

Patricia was disappointed that evening because the idea had rather tickled her. Fortunately, she hadn't started drawing. I prepared a union meeting announcement without illustration. Deprived of newsworthy material, all I could do was restate material from previous leaflets.

Over the weekend, I suggested a different illustration, inspired by comments from the Detroit radio host: the meeting at Mohawk's corporate office when they'd decided to launch the decert. Executives would be sitting around a conference table, each with a comment I'd provide.

"I don't know when the Board's going to issue its decision, but I'll need this ready the day it happens."

Patricia was even more intrigued by this idea than the previous one. She spent hours online, researching pictures of conference tables, chairs, and management personality types. She established sitting positions and gestures for each figure, studying photographs portraying relevant postures.

Only a handful of loyal union members showed up at the March 28 shift meetings. I couldn't fault those who abstained from a presentation about how nothing had changed.

CHAPTER 11

Labor Board Decision

The committee and I had been drifting through *the doldrums* for two months as March meandered into April with no developments requiring a response. There were always details to review with Mike or Neil, while committee members called requesting updates I couldn't provide. Patricia's latest masterpiece was nestled comfortably in my hard drive, patiently awaiting its moment. Warmer weather was making its introduction and I wandered along my creek photographing trout lilies and dogtooth violets.

I called Neil on the morning of April 11 to address his remaining questions regarding our response to the employer's December charge. The review involved minor details and took only a few minutes.

"We made a determination on the union's charges earlier today," said Neil. "We found merit to some of the union's allegations but not all of them." He was very low-key as if making schedule arrangements. My heart was pounding.

"Which allegations did you go with?"

"We found merit to the allegations of employer solicitation, and also added counts of illegal interrogation, and surveillance of employees that occurred during the process."

This was the first time the Board had ever expanded the scope of my charges. I asked how he'd uncovered the additional evidence. Neil said he'd been interviewing witnesses on his own. He couldn't provide the names, other than to say agents had been following up with individuals mentioned in affidavits by union witnesses.

"What about *free rein*?" I asked.

"We found merit to that as well."

My heart was beating faster. *The damn brief had worked.*

Neil continued by noting the Board had found the employer promised benefits to workers if the union was decertified, and that one of the TV monitor postings violated the Act. I thought for a moment and asked if he could tell me which members of management were directly implicated.

"We found three *bad actors*: Margie Clemmons, Elise Griffin and Ray Santos."

Though considering it a stretch, I probed for leaflet content by requesting the number of violations between them. Neil pored through his notes and itemized twenty-seven "bad acts."

The agenda committee had not found sufficient evidence to prove the decertification had been launched during the Garner trip, or that several minor allegations could be substantiated. I asked if the union could go public but the agent requested we wait twenty-four hours. He hadn't been able to reach Fredrick and the employer had a right to be informed first.

"When will the decision be reduced to writing? I assume the petition is being dismissed."

"As you know, the Complaint will be a lengthy document but I expect it will be going out within the next two or three days. The petition will involve a separate process with the Regional Director."

I'd never seen a substantive complaint issued and the petition not dismissed along with it, but Neil told me that was how the Region wanted to proceed.

I hung up and called Mike. He shared my exhilaration about the added counts of management coercion, and especially the inclusion of our free rein evidence. Our case now rested upon a foundation of daily activity, seasoned with specific incidents of an extreme nature. We agreed to withdraw the rejected allegations. Region 10 would now evolve from being a neutral investigator into a joint-advocate in Mohawk's prosecution. It wouldn't be strategic to open a new front in which we contended against the agency.

Mike prepared a three-page position statement to Regional Director John Doyle, arguing for immediate dismissal of the petition based on precedent.

A *causation hearing* should not be held in this case. As the Board explained in *SFO Good-Nite Inn*, a *causation hearing* is only appropriate when "there is no straight line between the employer's unfair labor practices and the decertification campaign."

I typed our long-awaited victory leaflet, attempting to distill complex elements of the determination into a user-friendly presentation, followed by our latest cartoon.

The Labor Board alleges that the following members of management engaged in *27 counts of illegal union busting*:
Margie Clemmons *Elise Griffin* *Ray Santos*

The next time one of them talks to you about *"obeying the rules,"* let them know what **hypocrites** they are. Violating federal law is far more serious than disobeying plant rules.

I called committee members to share the news and the need to keep it confidential for a day. "Meet me after work tomorrow. There'll be a leaflet waiting."

I felt an overwhelming sense of gratitude toward our witnesses and arrived at the hall early to speak with Taina about preparing an award for each:

> Certificate of Appreciation
>
> For the courage to come forward
> and speak
> the Truth
>
> 2017/2018 NLRB Case
> against Mohawk's illegal union busting

I asked her to keep this a secret for now. I didn't want to give these out until the Complaint was in writing and the petition dismissed.

Committee members straggled in and we took our usual seats. Bill asked if I thought this was it, or if management would appeal and we'd end up at trial. "I don't see what's the point in them dragging this out," he said, "not with all the evidence we got against them."

"I hope you're right. Any other time I'd have agreed with you. I'm sorry all of this is so complicated but it is what it is." I stood, briefly making eye contact around the tables and continued. "Please bear with me and I'll try to make it as simple as possible."

Under normal circumstances, the smart move for the employer would be to fold their hand and move on. Mohawk might very well do that to avoid a labor dispute that dragged on for years. But Fredrick might have convinced them to look ahead at the big picture. If we beat them at trial, the case would end up being heard by the Board in Washington. By that time four out of five members would have been appointed by Trump. It was impossible to know how much the law and precedent might have changed by then.

"Is it ok if I ask something now, before I forget?" Darnell interjected, and I nodded. "Even if the law changes, isn't this case still bound by the law as it was when all this happened?"

I replied that was the million-dollar question. Our lawyers were still debating it. Even if we survived the Board, the company would get another bite at the apple before a U.S. Circuit Court of Appeals. "One way or the other, Fredrick lines his pockets in the process. Mohawk's stock sells for $280 a share. To them, it will all be chump change. But there's another hurdle as well.... Sorry, I said this was complicated."

The company might demand a causation hearing before the petition was even dismissed, forcing the union to prove how each violation increased the number of signatures. Ira and Mike were extremely concerned about this. Until now, such a hearing had only been used in situations where the complaint was limited to minor infractions. But conservatives were pushing for this to become a routine step in the process.

"But after all the shit they done, how can any idiot argue that it didn't affect the number of signatures?" asked Bill.

"The arguments will be made by idiots to the idiots who are now in charge," I said, reminding him that with one exception, none of our witnesses actually signed. We might have to prove how those who did sign were directly influenced, name by name. I instructed the committee to keep all of this confidential. For now we would put on a joyous face and celebrate our victory.

On Monday morning I received a frantic call from Jeff. "Justin wrote this letter! It's in everyone's mailbox where they live. He saying everything in our leaflet is lies."

"You're meeting me for a plant visit in a couple of hours. Bring it to the showroom."

I was running late and traversed the serpentine landscape of Hwy.

158 at seventy miles per hour, crossing solid lines to pass slower vehicles with my sandwich held in one hand. Jeff slipped me the letter as he opened the locked door between the waiting area and front office, informing me that Greg was already in the showroom.

I donned my safety gear and we walked the maze of aisles and machinery. "I still have no idea where I'm going," I whispered to Jeff. "If we got separated, they might find me a month from now, wandering about and starving to death."

Greg Lovett remained affable and we chatted about the history of carpet weaving as if the events preoccupying both parties were unfolding in another dimension. I told him my girlfriend was an artist and responsible for most of my knowledge on the subject. He turned toward me and asked if she was the one drawing the cartoons.

"Yes, she is."

Greg surprised me by answering, "I really like her work."

The exchange was yet another indication that while local production heads were following orders, they weren't overly invested in the dispute.

I arrived at the hall shortly before shift-change, in time to read the company's message to workers:

The union's decision to declare victory was **premature.**
Your petition is still alive and well!

- The decision announced yesterday by the NLRB **does not find** that the Company violated the law.
- Charges filed through the NLRB go through several stages, and **this is only the first stage.**
- Because these charges are about **blocking your right to vote**, the local NLRB office is required to send the case to Atlanta and Washington for a decision, and even that decision may not be final.
- There are also **charges against the union** that are still under review.
- Do not believe the union's propaganda. **You know your management team** better than that.

Once seated, I told the committee their questions from the previous week about Mohawk's intentions had been answered.

"I'll fight them for as long as it takes," said Bill. "If this goes on past my retirement age, I'll stay and see this through."

"See what I been telling you about Justin," said Darnell. "You don't know him like we do. He's right in the middle of this. Why else would he write that letter and send it to each employee in their mailbox?"

"I don't believe he wrote it. It's not his style of writing and I doubt he understands the case well enough. His business is rugs, not labor law. This was probably written either by Fredrick or someone at a corporate level, and he was told to sign it."

"Well, I don't believe that," said Thomas. "He's a snake in the grass and always wanted the union out of here."

I backed off. The worst mistake an organizer can make is defending a member of management in the middle of a fight. I shifted focus to practical considerations. We were going to need a full-court press on the shop floor to hold folks together and psyched for the long-haul.

We'd won a major battle but the war wasn't over. The day we ended up in front of a judge, the Complaint would lose most of its value. The union would be required to prove everything all over again and convince all our witnesses to show up for a trial they were told probably wouldn't happen. Our investigation would resume as we sought to identify new witnesses who didn't come forward the first time. It was imperative to keep the campaign high-profile and exciting enough to keep people involved.

"The problem is people are confused," said Bill. "They don't know who to believe anymore. The union says one thing and the company says something else."

That was of course the whole point of the letter, but whoever wrote it made a serious mistake. Fairly soon we'd receive the written Complaint. I'd run copies and the committee would distribute them throughout the mill. The rhetoric of both parties would no longer matter, because all discrepancies would be addressed by the United States government.

"The company will look like bigger liars than ever," I told them. "But for now, there'll be a leaflet to pick up tomorrow."

Thomas was a quiet, thoughtful man who didn't feel the need to be center stage. He'd worked at the mill for forty-nine years and when he offered a suggestion, it was worth considering. "What about stickers?" he asked. "The union used to give out stickers when we were in a fight with the company."

It was a good idea but it raised the question of how many people would wear them. Either way we'd be making a statement to management. A significant shop floor presence would generate a show of strength. But if fewer than half the workers wore the stickers we'd look weak, as if the majority wasn't behind us. I didn't want to risk it unless we could be reasonably sure.

"People gonna wear them," said Bill. "I know these folks. Even some of those that aren't in the union will wear a damn sticker if it's given to them."

I suggested having Patricia design a logo summing up our whole campaign: the classic red circle with a slash through it meaning *No*. Within, black lettering would say "Union Busters," so *No Union Busters*.

I'd print sufficient numbers to keep them in circulation for weeks. Everywhere a person looked they'd get our message. Management sometimes brought customers out on the floor and would be getting asked about the stickers by those to whom they were most accountable. Sometimes the most convincing arguments to end a labor dispute come from a company's customers behind the scenes, because they're afraid of disruption in getting their products on time.

"Can we get this put on T-shirts also?" asked Jeff. "We sometimes give out union T-shirts to our members."

This again raised the concern about how many people would wear them. A flashy shirt worn by 20 percent of the workers would present an embarrassing image. We'd need to give them to nonmembers as well.

"If you give these people a free shirt, they'll wear it," said Thomas. "Besides, some of these nonmembers supported us enough to be witnesses."

I asked Jeff if the local treasury had enough money to pay for it, as this would be a big item to put on my expenses. The local president assured me funds were available and it seemed a good time to wrap the meeting. "Leaflet starts going out tomorrow evening. Patricia will fast-track the artwork and I'll check on getting the shirts printed."

I drove home and wrote my rebuttal to Justin's letter before dinner:

Mohawk has been lying to you. Mohawk has been lying to the Labor Board. **The NLRB decision does find that Mohawk violated the law.**

We did make *one mistake* in our leaflet. We said the Labor Board found that Margie, Elise, and Ray committed 27 acts of illegal union busting. The Board just informed us that the actual number is **45 acts of illegal union busting**.

MOHAWK INSULTS YOUR INTELLIGENCE

We've got to assume that senior management *knows how to read*. Look at our last leaflet. We never said the petition had been dismissed. We said:

The Labor Board will next discuss *permanent dismissal of the petition* because of *illegal management involvement* and support.

We have no problem if people disagree with us. But don't put words in our mouth and then argue against them.

CHAPTER 12

Becoming a Test Case

On April 19, I had what I believed would be a routine phone call scheduled with Neil. "The Regional Director has made a decision to dismiss the petition," he told me several minutes into the discussion. The paperwork from Atlanta was expected shortly.

I prepared yet another leaflet for distribution the next day, titled *The Petition Is Dead*. It would be accompanied by stickers that had just arrived.

> The union didn't block the election. *The election was blocked by the United States Government* ... because it was based upon an unlawful petition.

My respect and appreciation for this committee continued to grow. The foundation of a victorious campaign is timing and momentum. I'd told the leaders we'd have to hit the ground running and never stop until we won. They'd all lived up to it. Our rhythm had never faltered for even a single beat because someone didn't hold up their end. The four men had sacrificed countless hours before and after work, usually with little notice. They were about to distribute their third leaflet within a week, on all shifts. I asked Taina to order plaques honoring their service, to be awarded at a victory dinner.

The following day, Region 10 issued a dismissal letter regarding most of the charges against the union, sent to RTW attorneys representing Daphne:

> You allege that ... members of the Union's executive board watched employees whom they believed were involved with the decertification petition.... Union agents did not speak to, threaten, or otherwise take any action as they allegedly watched these employees who were acting out in the open....
> A union is free to state its views on employees who support a decertification petition, as long as the statements are not accompanied by threats of reprisal.

The committee met again on April 24 and I asked how workers reacted to the leaflet and stickers.

"People loved them damn stickers," said Bill. "Some plastered several of 'em all over their clothing, including nonmembers. I heard some of them even ended up stuck on restroom stalls."

"That breaks my heart," I murmured with a touch of sarcasm.

Bill said management had posted a new message on its TV monitors, attempting to discredit our leaflet by claiming there hadn't been a final de-

cision. He believed only something in writing from the Board would let people know whom to believe.

"Hopefully that will come soon. Look, I hate to rain on everyone's parade, but the Board's finally reached the point where they're making a decision about everything, including the case against us."

I paused to allow everyone a moment to shift gears. Region 10 would be dismissing all of the company's allegations except for two ... the grievance meeting where committee members supposedly asked management to fire Daphne for circulating the petition, and the one about telling workers that people who circulated the petition would be fired.

"But all we were doing is trying to get the company to enforce its own rules," said Darnell.

I explained the Board had made its decision. Often when an agency sides with the vast majority of a union's case, they'll throw the company a bone to maintain the appearance of impartiality. The strategy can prove useful in a courtroom.

"No. This ain't right," argued the mill chair. "I wanna be able to take the stand and face my accusers."

I shared my discussion with Mike about our response to the upheld CB allegations. The Labor Board was going to join forces with us as they prosecuted Mohawk in federal court. We couldn't compromise that relationship by fighting against them in a different trial. The charges against us were insignificant by comparison. We'd sign a settlement agreement with the Board containing a non-admission clause and post a notice in the plant promising to withdraw the grievance in question and honor the rights of anti-union employees. Darnell's name wouldn't even be mentioned, because the charges were against the union as an institution, not specific individuals.

"They're still about lies people been telling about me and dragging my name though the mud. I can't go along with this," said Darnell, becoming increasingly adamant.

I assured him he wasn't being blamed for what might have been said. The disputed events occurred back in October before the committee received any training in these matters. Everyone was doing the best they could in an impossible situation. What mattered now was the big case and saving the local.

"Look, these charges against us are just piddly shit," said Bill. "There's no point in fighting them."

Darnell exhaled slowly and nodded. He then asked to be excused from the meeting early to take his boy to the doctor. I asked if he had a grandson staying with him.

"No. My wife and I adopted this little nine-year-old. He's autistic and would have grown up in an institution. He's a little white boy. My wife and I met him through our church and fell in love with him."

I was overcome by a new-found appreciation for the underlying love and devotion to service motivating our mill chair. It was extraordinary that a man approaching sixty years of age would make such a commitment.

On April 30, Region 10 of the National Labor Relations Board issued its *Consolidated Complaint and Notice of Hearing* against Mohawk Industries. The eleven-page decision cited each violation in detail. The employer was given two weeks to file its response and a trial was scheduled to begin on September 10 in the Winston-Salem hearing room.

I studied the complex document and wrote a leaflet to be attached once it was copied:

Finally! *The truth is out.* No need to wonder who to believe. Read what the National Labor Relations Board has to say after a six-month investigation....
To help you sort through it, here's a couple of tips:
- The *juicy stuff* is on pages 3 through 8
- We've underlined the beginning of important sections, or made a star next to the paragraph
- It took over two pages to list all 30 of Margie Clemmons' illegal acts
- Ray Santos was cited for 12 illegal acts
- Elise Griffin for 3
- The list goes on and on with violations committed by Mohawk as a company

Chapter 12. Becoming a Test Case

On May 2, the Region sent its formal dismissal of the petition to Daphne's RTW attorneys. A proposed Settlement Agreement was presented to the employer. It contained a posting to be displayed on all bulletin boards and TV monitors and read aloud to employees at group meetings. The document required an admission of guilt and strict compliance protocols.

Fredrick and RTW attorneys submitted objections to the Settlement Agreement, already signed by the union, regarding the remaining charges we faced. They argued that the Region had discriminated against the employer by requiring a more stringent settlement and that the union had "trampled on employee rights" and committed "hallmark violations."

On Saturday evening, Patricia and I joined committee members and their families for our victory dinner at Ruby Tuesday. I was delighted that after months of enjoying her artwork, they finally had a chance to meet her. She's a down-to-earth southern girl at heart who always got along well with union folks. Darnell brought his wife and adopted son, and Thomas his girlfriend. Bill was the last to arrive on a new motorcycle, explaining he'd have to leave early for an out-of-town biker party.

Once everyone was seated and introductions made, I asked the waitress to wait until we called her, and stood up to make my remarks. "I want y'all to know from the bottom of my heart that I've never worked with a finer group of people under fire."

Patricia continued chatting with Thomas's girlfriend seated beside her. I gently put my hand on her shoulder and whispered, "Please, I'm trying to speak." She glanced up with a startled and hurt expression.

"Don't worry about it," said Jeff. "He does that to us all the time."

I finished praising the committee for its efforts and handed out the plaques, saying we'd beaten the odds and won a major victory—especially impressive, given what was happening to unions across the country. For right now, we would stay positive and keep people focused on that victory ... allowing it to sink in and become real. The time to start discussing the trial would make itself known.

We ate and enjoyed each other's company for two hours, as Darnell's adopted son silently darted about with a tiny smile and shining eyes. Jeff remained behind after the others had left, holding his plaque and posing for Patricia's camera. "Maybe pretty soon we'll be hearing wedding bells," he said.

"Not for us," I replied. "We've been together nearly twenty-five years. If it ain't broke, don't fix it."

Part Two—The Case Unfolds

I was back in campaign mode. Winter's cobwebs were swept from my mind as I maneuvered under pressure with my back to the wall. Mohawk naturally responded with a series of TV monitor postings:

> The specialist the union hired knows exactly
> what to accuse the company of to get the
> NLRB to block your petition
>
> (*and in another*)
>
> We will continue to tell you the truth and we
> will present the truth to the judge, under oath

I in turn prepared a leaflet with the Dismissal Letter printed on back:

> The Company postings always give us a good laugh. They are such ***terrible liars!***
>
> * First they mail everyone letters, lying about the Labor Board decision, saying "the petition is alive and well."
> * The NLRB decision is put in writing and the union gives out copies.
> * Now all Mohawk can come up with is to say the union "specialist" is able to get the NLRB to do whatever he wants.
>
> Management proudly boasts that it will **commit perjury** in September.

Cartons of T-shirts arrived at the union hall, bearing the red and black *No Union Busters* emblem on a light grey background. I joined the committee on a reconnaissance mission to survey the best locations for a cumbersome distribution, given the heavy boxes and need for size selection. We agreed to station cars carrying shirts in all three employee parking lots.

Bill called the next morning from work. The security guard had pulled him and Darnell aside as they entered the plant gate at dawn. One of the department heads had approached the guard shack the previous afternoon as we surveyed parking lots after working hours. The guard had been instructed by him to call the police next time he saw us there conducting union business. I replied that while the union rep technically didn't have a right to be there, as employees the committee members did. I promised to consult Mike for a second opinion.

Mike responded that afternoon with case law supporting my position and I informed Bill. It didn't guarantee the police wouldn't be called during T-shirt distribution. The officer in charge would probably ask committee members to leave. If they didn't comply, the men would be escorted out in handcuffs for the matter to be sorted out later.

"Well, that's all right," said Bill. "I ain't afraid to get locked up."

Chapter 12. Becoming a Test Case

"It's not worth it. We'll use it as an opportunity to file new Board charges."

I asked Patricia to prepare another cartoon in time for an upcoming meeting announcement. It would be titled *The Three Outlaws*, displaying pictures of Margie, Ray and Elise wearing cowboy hats in an old west setting, making comments about the charges against them. Jeff sent Facebook photos to use as reference.

Fredrick, never one to be outworked by me, filed the generic employer appeal in response to the Complaint. Every statement in a complaint is considered an allegation, including background information preceding the pages of violations. I find it amusing how company lawyers gratuitously agree with the opening language before denying the actual charges:

> NLRB: At all material times, Respondent has been a corporation with an office and manufacturing plant in Eden, North Carolina, and has been engaged in manufacturing and the nonretail sale of carpets and rugs.

> FREDRICK: The employer admits the allegation in this paragraph.

Daphne stood at the plant gate on May 14, handing out her own leaflet. The rhetoric urged people to immediately withdraw from the union, citing complex legal rationale that would supposedly override the yearly *get out window* on membership cards. She bragged that she'd written the presentation.

The committee handed out our meeting announcement the next morning, with *The Three Outlaws* displayed across the bottom.

> The National Right to Work Committee has entered the fight on behalf of Daphne Little. They are the most **vicious, ugly** bunch of **hypocrites** in America today....
> The NRTWC wrote Daphne's leaflet. We have seen the same leaflet in many other plants.

Neil emailed the same day, announcing Field Attorneys Timothy Mearns and Brenna Schertz had been assigned the case, and all future communications should go to them. I called his cell to express appreciation for his hard work and attention to detail while digging deeper to expand the case with new witnesses.

There was a tickle in my chest as we spoke, that by night had turned into a cough that Robitussin couldn't suppress. I called my doctor the next day for a codeine-based prescription. It allowed me to sleep but I struggled through daylight without it.

I drove to Eden on May 17 for shift meetings, swilling over-the-counter

cough syrup and sucking on lozenges. My head was spinning as I rose to address the membership, willing the incessant bronchial irritation to remain dormant for a few hours. I hedged my bets by explaining I was sick.

"I promised I'd be here, so here I am. This is too important a meeting to miss."

I reviewed the complicated chain of events unfolding in rapid succession. "Most of the time when I get a complaint against a company, it's at best 75 percent of our most important charges. This is the first time we've ever gotten a complaint that's better than the charges I filed. Last winter I said we'd hold the line against the dark forces overrunning this country, and we did."

I was wracked by coughing and returned to my seat behind the table, praising the committee as the real heroes of our fight. If it hadn't been for the witnesses they'd identified and convinced to come forward, there would have been no charges to file. "We wouldn't be sitting here today because there probably wouldn't be a union."

As the members applauded, my efforts to subdue the cough failed again and I was overcome by another seizure. It was difficult being so vulnerable and out-of-control in public, but in the back of my mind, I realized my willingness to carry on in this condition offered a message more eloquent than words. I asked if someone from the committee could take over for a few minutes while I visited the restroom.

Chapter 12. Becoming a Test Case

I returned after regaining my composure and continued. My well-honed edge and psychic armor were gone, and all I could do was trust in the moment and speak from my heart. "The truth always comes to light in heaven, but it doesn't always win out in this world ... especially when the forces of deceit and corruption have all the money and power. But a group of working people here in Eden took a stand and exposed a Fortune 500 company for what it is."

I made it through the next meeting but asked the committee to run the last.

My recovery was unusually slow and I had to control my cough during an increasing number of radio interviews. A feature article in the county newspaper, *Rockingham Now*, was the most strategic coverage because of its broad community presence. The committee got its picture in the publication. Margie Clemmons' wanton disregard for federal law was revealed to members of the church in which she's active. Reporter Gerri Hunt asked for my overall philosophy on collective bargaining:

> I tell companies that no union, on its worst day, busts your chops half as bad as your own customers. Companies negotiate terms and conditions with their customers and suppliers. In the middle is labor. It's really no different to negotiate terms and conditions with your workforce, the people who turn supplies into products.

Jeff and I toured the plant on May 23. Our ability to walk the aisles and greet employees in the midst of hostilities offered a more potent statement about the union's power and determination than rhetoric from either side. Margie Clemmons once again shadowed our movements but never lingered to engage. *No Union Busters* T-shirts and stickers were visible throughout the entire building.

The committee and I held our customary meeting following a plant visit. "The people loved that last cartoon," said Bill as we took our seats. "They were standing around in little groups at the gate when we gave out the leaflet, pointing at the pictures and saying, 'There's Margie, that's Ray.'"

"Who do they believe now?"

Bill replied that finally seeing our message in the words of the United States government had tipped the balance and proven management had been lying from the start. People had of course witnessed anti's running around the plant during October with the petition, being assisted by Margie and Human Resource directors, but reading the government documents made it real.

Part Two—The Case Unfolds

I discussed the latest news: two United States attorneys had been assigned to the case. The lead attorney was named Tim and a woman named Brenna would serve as second chair. I'd never been involved in a case where the Board assigned two lawyers. Given their current budget and staff cuts, it showed how much this trial was being prioritized. Other than calling to introduce myself, there hadn't been much contact yet. But from this point on, it wasn't really the union's case anymore. Mohawk would be prosecuted in federal court by the United States government and we'd assist them.

"Our last leaflet was it for a while," I told them. "If you think this has been a vicious fight during the complaint phase, you ain't seen nothing yet. Mike doesn't want us to risk putting anything in writing that can be used against us in court."

"Should we be going about the plant then, letting people know what's going on and getting them ready for the trial?" asked Darnell.

I responded we should let our victory keep sinking in and raising morale. It would take some people longer to digest than others. The union was also in an awkward position. We'd convinced some of our witnesses to come forward by telling them their affidavits would remain confidential and a trial wasn't likely. Neil had told them the same thing. No one was lying. The odds of something like this being appealed and ending up in court were slim. It was going to be a shock to some of our folks.

"So why do you think it's happening this time?" asked Thomas.

I suggested Fredrick had convinced Mohawk that by going the distance, they'd have a chance at a reversal once it got to Washington. But it was far more complicated. Even if Mohawk decided to settle, the Right to Work lawyers might litigate the case on behalf of Daphne. Though we viewed her as the company's pawn, the law now considered her a separate party.

"Right to Work doesn't really give a damn about Daphne or even whether we have a union here in Eden. They have bigger fish to fry ... on a national and legislative level. Their goal is to undermine the entire labor movement by changing laws and eliminating the very rights our Complaint is based on. They're recruiting and using people like Daphne all over the country."

On May 30, Fredrick Englehart filed a brief before the NLRB in Washington, requesting a review of the Regional Director's dismissal of the petition. The twenty-five-page document described John Doyle's decision as "arbitrary and capricious," based solely upon "false, yet sworn

126

statements … by Union in-plant employee-supporters" and taking "union hyperbole" at face value. He extolled the employer's virtues and noted, "Notwithstanding the facts, the Union regularly demonized Mohawk." He cast Daphne as a champion of "employee rights" besieged by union thugs.

The attorney sought to discredit the union by offering passionate arguments against two of our withdrawn allegations, while failing to address the management solicitation and free rein violations at the heart of the Complaint. He invested several pages revisiting his theory that filing the second offer of proof *shortly after* the amended charge should override six months of investigation and accumulated evidence.

The brief was followed by fifty pages of exhibits, including transcripts from several of my radio interviews. Fredrick presented out-of-context sound bites as evidence that:

> "The supporting charges are all the product of one imagination…. According to that one imagination…"

> There is no such thing as a decertification campaign that really gets off the ground and results in a petition that's not employer conceived, dominated and driven.

> I had like 36 hours initially to file charges, file an offer of proof, get the petition blocked. We did it and then had a couple of weeks to deliver the witnesses and the folks came through.

The company lawyer sought to reverse our *truth versus lies* characterization of the conflict. "The Union's 'special projects coordinator' … expresses no interest in the truth or for an investigation *whether or not* the petition was, in fact, 'employer conceived, dominated and driven.'"

He concluded by asking the Board to resume processing the petition and "overrule its *blocking charge policy.*"

Three attorneys for the National Right to Work Committee filed a brief the same day titled, *Petitioner Daphne Little's Request for Review.* They also depicted their client as a champion of democracy thwarted by union coercion. Their primary focus was asking the Board to make this their long-awaited test case for repealing the *blocking charge policy*:

> This is a case of nationwide importance … and will have long-term effects on any decertification process in the future.

On May 31, Region 10 denied objections that the union had received preferential treatment in its settlement language, on grounds that charges against the employer were "egregious in nature." They agreed in principle with Bill that the charges against the union were *just piddly shit* by comparison:

> The employer also points to allegations that the Region dismissed. Inasmuch as we found no merit to those allegations, they have no bearing on the appropriateness of the settlement.

CHAPTER 13

Union Lawyers

On June 1, Patricia and I drove to Atlanta for the annual Southern Regional Joint Board conference. The six-hour stretch of I-85 is one of the most boring thoroughfares in America and I was grateful for her company. I forgot to factor in Friday evening traffic once we hit town and cut in and out of the EZ Pass lane when instinct told me police weren't around.

We arrived at the Crowne Plaza in time to unpack, and then headed down to the lobby. I wore my standard business casual getup of sports jacket with dress shirt and black khakis hanging over cowboy boots. Patricia is a natural performer who knows how to doll herself up to become an attractive complement to my public image. She'd been attending conferences for much of my career and had almost as many friends to greet as me. We ran into Jeff and I told him to prepare remarks because we'd be addressing delegates the next day.

I set up my customary display table by the convention room entrance to sign books and simply be accessible to friends and colleagues gathered over thirty years. There was no reason to attend the evening session, where people would spend two hours stating their name and local union affiliation. A young man with short black hair and a reasonably fit build, wearing a blue dress shirt and jeans, approached. He introduced himself as Mike Schoenfeld, the attorney who had taken over the case.

"I didn't know they let people like you into places like this," Harris Raynor joked as he shook my hand and moved on. I hugged local presidents who'd served with me in bygone battles, and enjoyed a surprise reunion with legendary attorney Dave Prouty, once our national union's general counsel and now working directly for SEIU. Ira stopped by and we agreed to meet the next day.

I awoke exhausted, with a cloudy mind, but adrenaline kicked in once elevator doors opened on the first floor and people approached to greet me. Harris opened the session with a review of the previous year's triumphs and challenges, after which I left to join Patricia for breakfast in the hotel restaurant. An endless succession of tedious conferences had left me insufferably weary of yuppie politicians extolling their solidarity with working people, about whom they knew virtually nothing.

I glanced inside the meeting, saw that none of my friends were speaking, and wandered about until I found Ira standing in-conference with two staff members. Mike had left to spend the weekend with his wife and two young children. Ira saw me approach and turned to shake my hand. The veteran attorney is a short, slender man, his balding head partially covered with wisps of longish white hair. His wrinkled face is both scholarly and elfin. He was dressed in a light blue business shirt, tan khakis and sandals.

"How worried are you about the briefs filed by Fredrick and RTW?" I asked.

"I'm very worried," said Ira and then elaborated: Opposing counsel was telling the Board's conservative majority exactly what it wanted to hear and laying foundation to use our case as basis to change the law. One of the revisions being considered in Washington was elimination of the *blocking charge policy*, meaning that decertification petitions would automatically result in an immediate election. If unfair labor practices were under investigation, ballots would be impounded and counted after final disposition of the case.

I noted that under these circumstances, the local union would erode and dissipate during several years of uncertainty. If charges were ultimately decided in the union's favor, the employer could still ask for a causation hearing to prove direct correlation between the violations and three-year-old signatures.

Ira cited research documenting that when a person is forced into doing something they didn't support, their attitude toward that issue ultimately becomes more positive. It meant a person signing a tainted petition, thereby committing themselves to an anti-union stance, was likely to vote against the union in an election. "However you look at it, this isn't a pretty picture."

Jeff rose to the occasion while addressing the delegates, offering a passionate and articulate account. He wore his *No Union Busters* shirt and presented one to Harris. I praised the committee for their valiant efforts and focused on our victory, rather than the challenges ahead.

I remained at my table during the afternoon's delegate workshops. Harris took a seat beside me. "All three lawyers and me went over every word of your interviews in Englehart's brief. None of us found anything illegal. But how about discussing something else in your next interview?"

"Look, it's what the radio hosts want to talk about."

Patricia snapped photos with her camera throughout the conference and took one of Jeff wearing his T-shirt.

On Sunday morning I headed north through the complex network of highway interchanges out of Atlanta, leading to the endless miles of I-85 Georgia. "It was a pleasant surprise seeing Dave Prouty again," said Patricia. "I asked what he thought of Mike and Dave said, 'He's a real pit bull.' I shared this with Mike and he seemed flattered."

Local 294-T president Jeff Totten at the 2018 Southern Regional Joint Board Conference.

I was proud that Patricia could fit into my world. I wouldn't have taken most of my former girlfriends within a thousand miles of it.

Ira returned to New Jersey and prepared a fifty-five-page brief responding to the May 30 filings by Fredrick and RTW attorneys. He noted Mohawk never disputed that its unlawful support required dismissal of the petition under current law. Instead it sought to have established policy overturned:

> The employer may not ask the Board to nullify its published regulation casually through ad hoc decision-making. Because the Policy is codified in the Board's Rules and Regulations, §103.20, to eliminate the Policy the Board must invoke APA rulemaking.

He referred to a formal procedure for government agencies to seek rule revisions, which could only be applied to future cases. Ira also turned our opponents' belabored arguments of favoritism against them:

> Bizarrely, Mohawk presents the Regional Director's rejection of several Union charges as somehow impugning the investigation's quality.... But the Director's

rejection of these charges reflects only favorably on the investigation's quality. It shows that the Director did not accept at face value Southern Region's evidence and that he gave serious consideration to Mohawk's evidence and argument.

I received a draft for review and input which was then forwarded to Mike with the understanding it would be returned to me for further comment.

During the same period, Fredrick Englehart filed a brief before the Board in Washington, appealing John Doyle's "abuse of discretion" and "discriminatory" approval of the union's Settlement Agreement. It was followed by transcripts of five radio interviews:

> the Union regularly distributed leaflets attacking the petitioner and one Union spokesperson appeared on YouTube periodically and attacked her.

During the course of his busy schedule, Fredrick, in good conscience no doubt, overlooked the fact that my remarks about anti-union employees were generic in nature and never once directly referenced Daphne Little.

On June 20, Ira's brief was returned to me with Mike's revisions. During my review, I came to a section itemizing the employer's violations and had second thoughts about one of my edits:

> Clemmons not only made multiple attempts to solicit and coerce signatures from three employees who worked closely together, but pressured them by stating that if one signed, they all would sign.

I became concerned the specificity might identify *the three girls* and subject them to further coercion as we prepared for trial. I decided to email Mike for his opinion but found a message from him instead, copying me on his filing of the brief. I called immediately.

"You're right, I was supposed to give you time for edits, but I'm working on another situation and wanted to get this out. Why? Was there something you wanted to add?"

I shared my thoughts.

"So you're afraid we may have outed the girls? Let me look through the brief.... I see what you're referring to. We might have gone into more detail than we should have. But there's nothing we can do now."

I told him it was otherwise an extraordinary piece of work and these things happen.

Mike called again at 6:30. The young, tough-minded attorney was talking through a haze of exhaustion and stress. "How bad do you think it is? Do you think we really outed the girls? I should have given you a chance to look at it again."

I told him not to worry about something already done. The thing everyone in the labor movement fears most is screwing up ... spinning out about a mistake and wondering if it will undermine everything. I'd been there myself. But none of us can walk on water forever without getting our feet wet. "Let it go. Have a good weekend with your family."

I touched base with Neil on Monday about the CB charges, now that the Settlement was being appealed, and used this as an opportunity to feel him out about the trial. I as yet had no relationship with the two young prosecutors and Neil had gradually taken me into his confidence. He told me Daphne wasn't looking forward to the trial. During their last conversation, she'd admitted to "hating this" and didn't want to be involved anymore. If she were to waive her right to have the petition reinstated should the company prevail at trial, Mohawk would probably settle.

Neil referred to the Board's policy of considering the petitioner a free agent, with final discretion regarding the petition submitted in her name. I asked about the procedure he mentioned and was told Daphne would simply fill out a form.

"Have you spoken to her about this?"

"No, but I have raised it with her Right to Work attorneys."

"And what do you think are the odds that they've passed it on to Daphne? They're using her to service their own agenda and settlement is contrary to their interests."

"I can't disagree with that, but we have to go through her counsel now that she's represented. By the way, please don't mention any of this to the committee."

There was no reason not to discuss it with the union's attorney. I asked about inviting Daphne to have dinner with me at Ruby Tuesday. She just might be curious enough to take me up on it, and the worst that could happen was "being rejected for a first date." But if she showed, I could let her know that filling out the form was an option to end all of this. I wouldn't pressure or even advise her, just let her know she had that choice. In the likely event her RTW lawyers had failed to raise it, she'd have one more reason to be pissed.

"It's a bad idea," said Mike. "We don't want you anywhere near the petitioner before the trial. She could just as easily portray you in court as having tried to coerce her into withdrawing the petition."

I acknowledged his concern and asked when he thought we should start prepping witnesses for trial. Mike replied that August would give us plenty of time, but we'd have to coordinate with the two Board lawyers so we could all be present. He'd spoken with Tim Mearns several times, mainly reviewing broad strokes of the charges and some of our legal arguments.

I met with committee members the next day to provide an update on the recent legal activity and begin focusing them on realities of the upcoming trial. There are few lines I won't cross in defending union members, but honoring confidentiality is a boundary I hold sacred. Rather than share what Neil confided about Daphne's disaffection, I decided to ask the guys directly about talk in the plant.

"Some people are saying they wish the union would quit pushing this already, and let things go back to normal," said Bill. "I keep telling them it ain't the union pushing it. It's Mohawk that keeps pushing things by appealing the decision and wanting to go to trial. It ain't the union's damn case no more. It's the government's case now and they decide what to do with it."

I asked how people were responding to this advice and was told they usually just listened. Bill noted that most of this was difficult for them to understand.

Darnell said there were numerous rumors of a plant-closing circulating on the shop floor. This illegal fear tactic is an employer's last refuge when the union's status is in question. Ray Santos had told numerous employees the plant would shut within the next couple of years, but without overtly connecting it to the union or trial. It appeared he was being well coached.

The mill chair provided another example. A woman working third shift had informed Kevin McCain of a rumor that the plant would shut right after the trial. She'd heard all our work would be transferred to a plant in Virginia making the same products, and that was how Mohawk would finally get rid of the union.

I asked the committee to investigate and attempt to identify the source. The rumor was of course ludicrous on its face. Some of the rugs manufactured in Eden were unique, along with the equipment producing them. But management was making every effort to demoralize workers as the trial approached. Frightened people don't show up in court and make good witnesses.

I inquired if anyone had heard what Daphne was adding to the mix. The four men remained silent for a few moments. "I ain't been hearing nothin,'" said Bill. "First time since all this started she seems to have quit running her mouth."

I discussed what had turned into a positive development regarding the charges against us. Fredrick's appeal of the union's Settlement Agreement would delay our posting in the plant for months. It was a stupid tactical decision on his part. It would have made us look bad to post first, before the trial. Even though the alleged offenses were minor, the company would have played it up. He'd bought us time with an appeal he couldn't win. Sometimes our enemies do us the best favors.

"How much money do you think he got paid for filing that appeal?" asked Thomas.

"More than you're gonna earn all month."

I excused myself to visit the restroom. As I neared the commode there was a sudden loud crash. I looked down to see a bottle of cleaner in the water, then glanced up over my shoulder to the supply shelf, where I made eye contact with a slender, black viper, its body coiled. My first impulse was wishing I had my camera to take advantage of this rare proximity to a serpent. Sensing my lack of fear, the snake concluded that perhaps discretion was advised, and slithered up a pipe through its entry hole. I found a roll of paper towels and plugged the opening.

When I returned to the committee's table, Jeff and Bill were preparing to leave but the Meadors brothers remained seated. I described the snake incident and Thomas said, "Elise is like a snake. On the outside she might seem all sweet and cuddly, but underneath there's a snake and she'll bite you when you least expect it."

The conversation digressed into an exchange of reptile encounters. "I have a blind turtle," I told them. Both men looked up at me, trying to digest this unexpected revelation from their union rep. I offered more detail:

In 2014, Patricia was driving down a two-lane highway and discovered a turtle run over by a car. His shell was crushed, forcing his eyes to rupture. She brought him home so he could at least die in peace, not getting cooked alive on hot pavement or run over again. I put some leaves and branches in a carton to make him more comfortable.

The next morning I expected to find him dead, but he was actually a bit more alert. I did some research and found a clinic for injured turtles at N.C. State's School of Veterinary Medicine. A volunteer recommended putting him to sleep because even if surgery could repair his other wounds, blind turtles usually refuse to eat and slowly starve to death. But I looked at this turtle and all I could feel was he wanted to live.

I drove him to the clinic and picked him up a month later. He'd been named Gumbo by the veterinary students and his new home became a fifty-gallon tank left over from a previous pet. Every day we set him in a basin to bathe and drink, but he wouldn't eat. For two months, I'd hold him and talk softly, forcing his mouth open with a tool provided by the clinic, while Patricia managed to shove in a couple of small bites.

Then one magic day, Gumbo took a bite of food straight from Patricia's hand, and the rest is history. He became part of our family. I spend an hour every other day preparing his bath and then feeding him by hand. He responds to his name and several other words. Turtles are slow-motion creatures and feeding usually takes thirty minutes. After a while Gumbo starts playing with his food like a child. But when I say, *last call, Gumbo*, he takes one more big bite, because he knows that's it and he's going back to the tank. He's the only turtle in the world who knows what *last call* means.

"Maybe God sent him to you," said Thomas, "so he could touch and heal some part of you that was neglected and needed to be blessed."

"It's interesting you should say that. I was just telling Patricia a couple of weeks ago that we did save Gumbo, but maybe he also saved us."

"That's what I'm talking about!" exclaimed Thomas.

This would be the last time we met before the plant shut during the first two weeks of July. The textile industry is a cyclical business with summer often being the slow season. Most mills close for July Fourth week and sometimes the next. I wished the men a good vacation and opportunity for rest as we locked up.

Two days later Mike forwarded an email from Tim Mearns saying he wanted to meet with all our witnesses over the next two weeks. It was time for me to insert myself into the relationship. I called Tim and after some initial pleasantries cut to the chase.

The plant was shutting for the next two weeks and most of the workers would be on vacation. If we expected our witnesses to cooperate, it was essential to honor their personal needs. A lot of folks were going to the beach with their families and wouldn't be returning for a day to meet with us.

"Well, we're on a timetable," said Tim "and we'd like to meet with as many people as possible during this period."

"You've seen the quality of our affidavits. The problem is some of our best witnesses are nonmembers and it took a lot of coaxing to get them this far. We've got to handle them with kid gloves. Bugging them during their vacation isn't the way to do it. These people have spent the last six months working in a factory. You've got to trust me on this."

Tim finally agreed to prepping witnesses during the second half of July and meeting reluctant individuals in Eden. Mike and I would travel to Winston for an introductory meeting on July 17, followed by committee interviews the next day.

I asked if Mike and I could attend subsequent prep sessions and was told Mike would be allowed to prep with committee members and shop stewards because they were agents of the union. But union representatives couldn't be allowed in any of the other meetings. This represented another significant policy change. I'd been an active participant during witness prep for other trials.

I then inquired how many days each of the witnesses would have to be in Winston-Salem during the hearing, expressing the assumption that people would only have to be present on the day scheduled for their testimony.

"Not necessarily," said Tim. "We may need to keep witnesses available for rebuttal. The government will put them up in a hotel for as long as we need them."

It was difficult to mask my annoyance while explaining the obvious: Most of these people had families and some worked second jobs. They weren't going to abdicate their primary responsibilities to be at our disposal. In my experience, the Board held trials at the courthouse closest to a plant's location, and I wanted to know why we weren't doing that for this case.

"That's not our current policy," he responded.

"What if we applied for a change of venue, in the interests of being able to produce our witnesses so we can actually have a trial?"

Tim responded that while he couldn't guarantee the Regional Director's response, we were welcome to try. However, even if we were successful, the employer would also have to sign off on it. I got back with Mike and he agreed to request the change of venue. He was surprised about not being allowed to sit with witnesses being prepped by government attorneys, noting he'd never had this problem at the Board's Atlanta office. It meant we'd have to schedule our own prep sessions during August.

"How many meetings do you think we can get these people to come to, in addition to a fuckin' trial?" I asked.

CHAPTER 14

Preparing for Trial

There was no work to be done during July Fourth week. All the attorneys were on vacation. But the explosion of nature on my property kept me from being bored. Patricia had talked me into setting up a 400-square-foot garden when I retired. To my astonishment, I came to love working the soil and was now a master at growing cucumbers. The campaign had taken precedence this year and caused a late planting, but the seedlings were several inches high and I carefully nurtured each one toward maturity under the relentless summer sun. Rare and exotic amphibians breed on my property and I spent hours photographing the first hatchlings.

On July 9, Elise responded to my request for the committee to be off work the following Wednesday, when I planned to present them in Winston-Salem:

> Our plant is shut until 7/16/18. A better time would be during shut down, because there would be no need for them to miss work. As we are returning back to production after a two week shutdown we are not able to release these employees due to production needs on that date of 7/18/18 at 11 a.m.

I can't believe it took them this long to stop cooperating with our witnesses, I thought and hit the reply button:

> The union does not require the services of the executive board this week. It's my understanding that the plant will have lighter than usual production needs this summer, due to soft market conditions.

> Please describe the specific market conditions on July 18 at 11 a.m. that will make it impossible for the company to release the requested employees, per Article 16 of the CBA.

Tim agreed to prep the committee after work at the union hall on July 18. Mike wrote John Doyle requesting the trial be moved to the Rockingham County Judicial Center, located several miles from the plant. He cleverly appealed to the interests of all parties, noting decreases in employee hardship, agency expenses, and impact on plant operations. He'd already pitched this to Fredrick and gotten approval.

Chapter 14. Preparing for Trial

We soon discovered that the Judicial Center was booked the week of September 10, as was another nearby courthouse. The parties agreed to investigate less traditional venues and after several unsuccessful attempts, Tim made arrangements at Rockingham Community College. John Doyle ordered the change of venue.

Abstaining from contacting the rank and file during their two-week vacation was one thing, but the committee needed to stay in the game. The following week would require a concerted effort to convince and schedule witnesses on short notice. I emailed talking points along with a list of six days offered by Tim during the second half of July:

POSSIBLE DAYS TO PREP

Are any not good for you? (Keep a notepad with you. Write down the bad days for each witness.)

I spent hours on the phone with each committee member, reviewing the materials. We'd been deprived of the normal two-week lead time I'd have used to schedule witnesses and communicate what some would perceive as an unwelcome message. The committee would once again have to go from zero to sixty in five seconds flat, with no margin for error. The witnesses were divided among the four men based upon work areas and relationships. Everyone agreed that the change of venue would make their task a lot easier. I couldn't believe Fredrick had actually agreed to it. He understood our people even less than I thought.

Mike forwarded an email from Tim, with copies of subpoenas served on two union stewards who were witnesses. I immediately called our attorney and was grateful he picked up. It was incomprehensible that subpoenas had been issued before we'd even had a chance to talk with workers.

I suggested Mike have a lawyer-to-lawyer discussion with Tim, requesting he hold off on further subpoenas to avoid thoroughly alienating everyone before we'd even begun to prep. It hadn't yet sunk in that affiants would now be required to show up in court and if we didn't pave the way, the government's approach would only intimidate them. Mike agreed to reach out, indicating he was equally stunned.

I expressed further concern that the subpoenas referred to government compensation of $40 per day, without mentioning the union's policy of paying for the rest. I could envision witnesses saying, *Why the hell should I put myself through all this and lose money in the process?* Tim needed to comprehend the imperative of the union explaining things first, in language our people could understand.

Mike called a few hours later and said that Tim and Brenna would refrain from issuing additional subpoenas. Justin emailed on Saturday, granting union leave to Jeff and Bill, but explaining in detail why the Meadors brothers couldn't be excused during start-up week.

The plant re-opened on Monday and I called committee members that afternoon to inquire about their progress contacting witnesses.

"I didn't get to see the girls today," said Bill. "The department had me running flat out starting up the looms. I don't usually cross paths with them. They work in a completely different part of the plant, but I'll try to get here early enough tomorrow to catch them on the way in."

Jeff and Thomas each had a couple of positive responses. Darnell had spoken to everyone on his list and each one had committed to the day of their choice.

My job description requires the ability to gracefully navigate onslaughts of unexpected developments. But everyone has their thresholds. I reminded Darnell that he'd been asked to find out which days *wouldn't work* for each person. What if ten people had all chosen Thursday? Even if the company allowed them off work, we'd be meeting with lawyers until 2 a.m.

I was trying very hard to swallow my stress and remain polite. He wasn't a professional and had volunteered countless hours. I apologized for the imposition but requested he go back to his folks and note only their *unavailable* days.

It was time to pack and drive to Eden for four nights at the Hampton Inn but I called to cancel the reservation. Adding two hours of travel to my workday felt more merciful than lying in a hotel bed, watching TV reruns until I was tired enough to attempt sleep.

Mike drove from Atlanta the next morning and we met in the NLRB parking lot at 1:30. Tim Mearns and Brenna Schertz were waiting in a conference room, where we greeted each other with polite handshakes and introductions. Tim was a short, slender man, with bangs curving across his forehead from an otherwise conservative haircut. He looked even younger than Neil. Brenna was somewhat heavyset though attractive and appeared to be about the same age. Everyone was dressed business-casual and I was the only one in a sports jacket. The suit-and-tie days for a meeting of this stature were long past.

"I thought it would be useful to give you an idea of the people behind the affidavits," I began, "and the best ways to approach them. Have either of you ever worked with a textile plant?"

They both said no, and I continued, describing it as a subculture unto itself, especially when dealing with people who'd been employed at a mill for a generation or two. It was a very cloistered existence. Most of our folks had spent their entire lives in the Eden area and had limited understanding of how the world worked. They harbored a patent distrust of outsiders, and beneath tough exteriors, were terrified of authority.

"Why are you telling us this now?" Brenna interrupted. "We're here to discuss the case and schedule witnesses. We plan to start calling them tomorrow to make appointments."

"I'm trying to explain why that's a bad idea. There's a process we went through to deliver these witnesses in the first place, and that process has to be continued by people they know and trust. I need to organize the scheduling. I drove them to Winston-Salem during the complaint phase and they'll expect me to do the same now."

"That won't be necessary," said Brenna with growing exasperation. "You're not going to be allowed in the meetings anyway."

I told the government lawyers I'd be there anyway, to provide continuity and moral support. This was my world and I knew it. I'd had boots on the ground for thirty years and gotten complaints issued at numerous textile operations. Their nice tidy stack of affidavits would mean nothing if key witnesses didn't show up in court.

"We will be issuing subpoenas at some point," said Tim.

"And what are you going to do to enforce them? This isn't the trial of John Gotti. We both know the Justice Department isn't on-tap to enforce Labor Board subpoenas."

"That's true," Tim acknowledged.

"Let's get back on track," said Brenna. "We're the attorneys prosecuting this case and we know how to do our jobs. You need to step out of the way and let us do what we have to."

"Look, I understand you're the attorneys handling the trial. But I'm the lead organizer on this project." I paused and stared into Brenna's eyes.

"Oh," she responded as if this were a new consideration.

I promised to avoid stepping on their toes regarding how the trial was handled and requested reciprocal consideration when it came to dealing with our people. If we both took responsibility within our areas of expertise and worked together, this would evolve into a formidable case.

"I think it's clear that we all have something to contribute," said Mike, diplomatically addressing the two Board lawyers, then changing the subject. Tim had recently told me not to communicate with Derrick Moss, one of our key witnesses, about the hearing. Our lawyer asked the reason behind this unusual request.

Tim explained the Complaint alleged that Moss solicited signatures from co-workers at the instruction of management, technically making him an agent of the employer. The government therefore planned to schedule his involvement through Fredrick Englehart.

"You've got to be kidding," I said. "He was coerced into doing that and provided an affidavit to that effect. He's one of our best witnesses."

Tim reiterated that nonetheless, the wording of the Complaint could be interpreted to consider Moss a company agent, and as such he was technically represented by their attorney.

"That's one key witness down before the game begins," I told him.

"Phil and I will review this and get back with you," said Mike.

Tim said the Board would like to be done prepping all witnesses by month's end. A second and more detailed prep would be scheduled a week or two before trial. He was inclined to give me a shot at scheduling witnesses, but if unsuccessful, would take over and follow customary procedures. I accepted this as a fair arrangement. If my efforts failed, I would want them to try another approach. All I cared about was winning the trial with an award strong enough to survive an appeal to Washington.

I then reviewed my list of potential witnesses with compelling testimony who'd refused to go on-record. I asked if any had been interviewed by Neil and if not, was it their plan to follow up. We were still permitted to add witnesses at this stage of litigation.

"We can't go into detail about witnesses the union didn't present, but rest assured, we know who these people are."

Mike and I stood in the parking lot on a warm summer evening and while tossing my sport jacket in back of the car, I asked what he thought of the meeting.

"I think we can work with them. You ruffled their feathers a bit but that's OK. I'll smooth things out if necessary."

I told him that I'd never encountered this type of jurisdictional arm-wrestling with Board attorneys. They were always grateful for my assistance. Paris Favor and I had worked hand-in-hand prosecuting Highland Yarn. We didn't even have a union lawyer present. I was in essence second chair.

Mike responded they were young and this was a new day, then asked if I was headed home or wanted to have dinner. He shared my taste for Indian food and I mentioned there was a great place in Winston.

Chapter 14. Preparing for Trial

Twenty minutes later we were relaxing in one of my favorite restaurants, ordering from waiters who barely spoke English. The traditional dishes were too succulent for us to be distracted by conversation. Once the table had been cleared we turned our attention back to the trial.

"The company's whole case is going to be focused on coming after you," said Mike. "Fredrick hates your fucking guts." He noted the employer didn't have any evidence to rebut our witness testimony about management involvement. Instead, they would try to discredit our witnesses by portraying me as someone who scripted the whole thing.

"Let 'em bring it on. I'd enjoy an opportunity to take the stand and face off against Fredrick and the Right to Work lawyers."

"I'd feel the same. You'll have a chance to come back at them any way you want. My guess is they'll be waiting on the courthouse steps and serve you a subpoena."

I asked if the court would require me to be sequestered along with other witnesses. The hearing would probably last two weeks. If I had to put on a suit and tie each morning, and then sit for eight hours in a waiting room, it would drive me crazy. I'd already been through this experience at the Highland Yarn trial

Mike said he couldn't offer any guarantee other than to strenuously argue I was essential to the proceedings and had the best understanding of our witnesses. He was sincere and down-to-earth, with the clean, unfettered killer instinct needed for our line of work. We sat around for another two hours exchanging war stories.

I called Bill while driving home and asked how he was doing.

"Not good"

"Why? What's wrong?"

"I managed to get up with Elma in the plant today. She said flat out she and the other girls don't want nothing to do with this. They don't want to be part of no trial and that's it."

"Did you talk to Annie or Lisa?"

"I didn't see them but what's the point after what Elma said."

Mike and I met at the union hall at 12:30 the next day to begin the arduous process of preparing for trial. We were joined by the two Board attorneys a few minutes later. Tim set up in Anthony's office while Brenna had to make do with the small, barely furnished room at the far end of the building. I figured the best way to remain in control of my case was to proactively organize logistics. I've never met a busy person who isn't seduced by having part of their job done for them.

Part Two—The Case Unfolds

The four of us convened in the larger office for a brief meeting. I laid out a confirmed witness schedule running from Friday through Tuesday and discussed ongoing efforts to get others on board. I informed the attorneys of Bill's discussion with *the three girls*, and promised he'd keep trying.

Brenna suggested calling them but I asked her to wait. They knew and trusted Bill, and to some degree me. We'd already been through this during the complaint phase. The women eventually came forward because they were pissed about how Margie tried to push them around. We should avoid being perceived as the ones now doing the pushing.

Brenna agreed to allow us a bit more time, noting that something had to be scheduled soon. I told her my next group was willing to come with me to Winston on Friday and asked if noon would work.

Tim surprised me by saying there was no need for us to come to their office. The attorneys had been authorized to conduct all interviews in Eden. He suggested 1 p.m. because they were meeting with "other witnesses" at a different location that morning. I assumed he was referring to witnesses Neil or the lawyers had discovered on their own. I was impressed that along with the change of venue, the Board had granted them a daily travel budget. Jeff and Bill sauntered through the heavy glass doors.

Brenna finished with Bill sooner than expected and I welcomed his company as I sat unoccupied at my table. "Did you have a chance to talk with the girls again?" I asked.

"No. I didn't see them this morning. I've got to be careful with all this going on. They work on the other side of the plant and I don't have permission to go anywhere near their department."

I re-emphasized they were the cornerstone of our case. We had a room full of people all subject to similar violations at different times, but *the three girls* were all hit by the same thing at the same time. They were nonmembers, so Fredrick would look like an idiot if he argued bias. Their collective story made the rest of our witnesses believable. In prior years, we'd have had enough to win without them. Perhaps we could still win the trial, but it would be far more difficult to survive an appeal to Washington.

"You have a unique gift," I told him. "Your strength is contagious, and you have the ability to pass it on to others. You used it once before with the girls. Try it again."

Jeff and Bill left before 3:00 and Mike joined the other two lawyers behind a closed door. The Meadors brothers entered and waited on a couch until Tim and Brenna emerged and chose their witness.

"I've been sticking up for you in there," said Mike. "Brenna's saying that you did a good job putting the case together but now you need to back off and let them handle it. I told them you understand this case better than anyone and we need you every step of the way. Hopefully I got through."

Mike drove home that evening, since would be no need for two people providing emotional support during the days ahead. The Board attorneys had other business the next day. I met with Thomas and a recently terminated employee named Calvin Grimes, who claimed to have shocking evidence of management involvement with the petition.

Thomas and Bill previously portrayed Calvin as a two-year employee who'd skated on thin ice since his first day. He was a hothead who routinely quarreled with supervisors and employees in his department. Some of his co-workers were genuinely afraid of him. Calvin had been terminated after reaching the final step of progressive discipline for refusing to wear his safety glasses.

Thomas entered the union hall shortly after 3 p.m., accompanied by a short but muscular black man in his twenties, sporting a goatee without mustache. Calvin sat across from me at the back table, while Thomas took his usual seat on the left wing of our formation. I decided to ask the young man about his information pertaining to the Board case, before delving into a personal grievance I already knew was a long shot.

Calvin claimed he'd been approached by a supervisor during October, and told Daphne wanted to meet with him in the front office. He walked upstairs and encountered the *petitioner* sitting behind a desk wearing business clothes. She clearly wasn't being paid to fulfill her normal responsibilities as an assistant weaver. Daphne asked why he was a union member, suggesting he revoke his membership and sign the petition. Calvin heard her out, then refused and returned to work. I sensed an underlying hostility and selfishness. This union member had waited eight months before coming forward with valuable evidence, until he found himself in trouble.

I turned my attention to the circumstances leading to Calvin's discharge. He offered a long-winded account of how his supervisor held him to a higher standard than others when enforcing plant rules. During the afternoon leading to termination, he'd been on break with a co-worker. Their supervisor approached as they sat on chairs outside the canteen, telling them to don safety glasses because they were technically "out on the floor." Calvin refused, rising to his feet and furiously proclaiming harassment and discrimination before walking off. He was proud of his manly stance, pointing out that failure to wear safety glasses hadn't resulted in discipline for other workers, including his friend during the incident in question.

Thomas stood and leaned over Calvin's chair, telling him that someone at the final stage of discipline should err on the side of caution when it came to insubordination. He lectured the young man in a fatherly manner, suggesting he was disliked by management and hourly workers because of his attitude. "You need to take responsibility and realize you brought all this on yourself," said the vice mill chair.

I told them we needed to examine the facts from a legal perspective. On its face, it appeared we were dealing with a classic example of disparate rule enforcement pursuant to just cause. I promised to make an information request to management, asking for Calvin's complete discipline record, including all notes and evidence used as the basis for termination. I privately didn't believe the whole story had been provided.

The Mohawk contract provides for a grievance procedure similar to most collective bargaining agreements. The aggrieved employee first meets with his supervisor and shop steward in an effort to address the issue. If unsuccessful, the grievant is represented by local officers before middle management, and finally the case is presented by the union representative to the plant manager and Human Resource directors. Cases involving discharge commence at the third step, as only senior management has authority to reverse termination. Unresolved grievances are subject to arbitration. I emailed Justin Scarbrough and Leslie Taylor, requesting a grievance hearing for Calvin.

I called Bill while driving home and found him in a better mood. "I got there early this morning and caught all three girls on the way in. Bopha was there with them. They all said they'd be at the hall tomorrow when they get off work."

I reached Tim on his cell and told him the timing was perfect. We had witnesses staggered to begin between 1:00 and 3:00. The *four* girls would be arriving at 4:15. I suggested we start on time. Just because they showed up didn't mean they'd wait around all night.

My preliminary meeting with Tim and Brenna went smoothly the following afternoon. The tension between us was gradually easing. We seemed to have arrived at a mutual appreciation for each other's hard work and competence, and our gears were starting to mesh instead of grind. The first witnesses arrived when scheduled and in good spirits.

I joined the attorneys in the larger office at 4:30. "It appears our wayward women haven't shown up," I said. Tim suggested it might be time for the lawyers to call them. I thought quickly, weighing the risks, and finally agreed. Perhaps the authority of U.S. attorneys would impress them.

I presented Bill with the news while driving home for the weekend. "They must have just been playing me at the gate," he said. "They just told me what I wanted to hear so I'd shut up and leave them alone."

There's a selfish side to everyone, no matter how committed to a good cause. One is either man enough to face it and stay real or compensates by ending up on the high horse of political correctness. Driving down familiar two-lane roads on a clear summer evening, I experienced my own humanity. The thought of putting so much work into this project, only to have it slip through my fingers because of reluctant witnesses, was intolerable. This possibility may have been a factor in Mohawk's decision to appeal.

Bill called on Monday morning, speaking more quickly than usual with urgency in his voice. "All our witnesses got subpoenas in their damn mailbox over the weekend. Even some people that weren't on our list got one. People are really shook up. There's some going around saying, 'I wasn't even a part of all this. Why the hell do I have to go to court?' Bopha got one and she's complaining that she told everyone from the beginning that she didn't want to get involved."

My heart was pounding and I immediately got hold of Mike. "I thought Tim told you they were going to wait on the subpoenas. What's their fucking hurry? The trial isn't 'til September." I told him the plant was buzzing like a hornet's nest. People were furious about being strong-armed and only receiving $40 compensation for their efforts. Fredrick couldn't have come up with a better strategy to undermine us.

Our lawyer was equally stunned, especially because he hadn't been given a heads-up. He couldn't guess "what the hell they were thinking" but promised to give Tim a call.

He got back with me as I drove toward Eden. Tim hadn't offered much of a response, only saying the Board had to move forward with its case. Mike surmised that someone higher up the chain of command wasn't interested in what we wanted and told him to go ahead and issue.

The scheduled witnesses showed up for their afternoon appointments and the committee straggled in when first shift ended. Jeff pulled me aside near the front door. Darnell had complained about me "bouncing him off the wall" the previous week, during our discussion about scheduling witnesses. He'd complained that no matter how hard he tried, he couldn't seem to do anything right. The president told me not to worry because he'd reasoned with the mill chair and calmed him down.

Part Two—The Case Unfolds

Once the committee was seated I stood up and backed away from the table to address the group. "I want to apologize to you if during the course of all this, I've stepped on anyone's toes and offended them. I've got nothing but respect for everyone on this committee. But when I go into overdrive I move very quickly, and sometimes get stressed and impatient with people I care about most. It gets me into trouble at home. It's just the way I am." I glanced around the tables and sensed my words had gotten through. "I understand the Labor Board attorneys went against what they promised and have been dropping subpoenas on people."

Darnell said even the anti's had been served. Robin had been telling people this was all the handiwork of Daphne and Elise, questioning why she had to appear in court. This would be interesting to explore on cross-examination when Robin took the stand. I asked the men to reach out to as many people as possible, letting them know we were as much blindsided by the subpoenas as anyone, and the union would make them whole for everything over $40.

Mike interrupted my monotony the next afternoon as I waited outside the prep sessions. Tim had received a complaint from management that I invited a witness to prep at the hall. The person was concerned about not knowing what to say in court and I supposedly told him, "Don't worry. I'll write it down for you."

I responded it was "total bullshit" and asked the identity of this supposed witness. Tim had described a tall white man with a ponytail but didn't offer a name. It sounded like Kevin.

"I never even met with him to prep," I said. "There's no need to prep people before their damn prep. Their affidavits are already on record."

Mike told me he was just keeping me in the loop and Tim didn't take the accusation "too seriously."

I returned to my state of sensory deprivation until Bill called. "I saw Annie at work today. She says she'll be there at the hall tomorrow evening."

"What about the other two"?

"I'm guessing if she actually shows up, the others will follow her lead."

I opened my laptop and tried to occupy myself on Wednesday after offering witnesses my greetings and assurances, and then watching them disappear behind closed doors. Later this afternoon would be put up or shut up time in regard to some of our best testimony.

Shortly after 3 p.m., Annie strolled into the hall and I met her at the door, thanking her for coming. She was earlier than expected because her department had gotten off sooner than usual, and the lawyers were still with other witnesses. Annie asked to wait outside and I decided to join her. It was a hot, cloudless day and we stood close to the building to be in the shade. I asked if Elma and Lisa were coming.

"I don't know. But I've been in court twice before and I know what I'm supposed to do."

She was wearing a light blue sleeveless shirt. I noticed she'd put colored streaks in her long wavy hair like a teenager and had a couple of discreet face piercings. "Your hair looks really cool," I said.

She smiled and I expressed my appreciation for how much her testimony had meant to the case. Annie shared that after twenty years, she'd finally paid off her mobile home.

I joined Tim and Brenna for our wrap-up session a couple of hours later and asked how Annie had done. Tim said she was "going to be fine." I apologized for the other two not joining her and asked how we'd handle it. They were still needed to provide corroboration. Brenna said the attorneys would be contacting them.

The shock of being subpoenaed had clearly made an impact on Annie, but I remained concerned about those who weren't persuaded. Neil had tried to subpoena someone during the complaint phase and it had gone ignored.

"We'll make multiple attempts to call them," said Tim. "But if all else fails, we'll put it in the hands of a federal marshal."

"You're telling me you've gotten authority to enforce these subpoenas?"

"Yes."

Tim concluded by noting the Complaint had been amended by removing language implying Derrick Moss was an agent of the employer. I was free to reach out and schedule his session.

On Monday, July 30 I received a call from Bill. "How come you didn't tell us the company gave up and the petition was pulled?"

"What are you talking about?"

"This morning all the department heads was called upstairs to a meeting. They came down about an hour later and pulled all the people in their area together in a group. My department head said the company wanted things to go back to normal and the petition had been withdrawn. It was pretty much the same thing with the others. Does that mean we're not going to court?"

"This is all news to me. If it's real, either Mike or I should have been notified by Tim. I'll call them both and get back with you."

Part Two—The Case Unfolds

I was relieved that Tim was available and I wouldn't have to spend hours of uncertainty waiting for a response. Tim acknowledged the news from the mill, saying Daphne had withdrawn the petition early that morning and he'd been planning to give me a call.

I expressed my assumption that the trial was off. Tim told me he'd forward a copy of the proposed Settlement Agreement sent to the employer in May. It still required Fredrick's signature. The attorneys would continue prepping for trial until the charges were settled. The discussion hardly seemed real. It was like preparing for a tornado, seeing the skies darken and funnel clouds approach, then suddenly it's gone and the sun is shining with birds chirping.

Mike was equally surprised not only by the news, but having not been contacted immediately, noting it was very strange getting the news from inside the plant. I followed up with Bill, verifying the petition had been withdrawn. The lawyers would continue prepping for trial until the actual violations had been resolved, but it was unlikely that wouldn't happen. Why go to court when there was nothing substantial left to fight over?

"What about the election?" he asked.

"The election was based on the petition. No more petition, no more election."

Bill asked if Right to Work lawyers would nonetheless carry on the fight. I told him no, they didn't care one way or another about charges against Mohawk. The attorneys were using Daphne and our whole situation as a test case to change the laws about decertification and would move on to other conflicts.

Fredrick and the RTW lawyers received a letter from Region 10 confirming the petition's withdrawal, and one from Washington declaring their appeals were now moot. I began contemplating the tone of my next leaflet. Fighting is a calculated means to an end. My intention was to parlay our victory into a renaissance of labor relations within the plant; not born of trust but rather necessity. If the committee used its newly discovered power to strategically build bridges, I believed Justin would be receptive.

WHERE DO WE GO FROM HERE?

The union would like to put this fight behind us and rebuild a productive bargaining relationship with the company. Textiles is a troubled industry, and we all need to work together to maintain the plant's success. This was a *really foolish time* for Mohawk to start a labor dispute!

It will take a long time before *trust* returns to our plant. But we need to move

150

forward one step at a time. There's no point in holding a grudge. But an ongoing peace will be a two-way street.

As we've been telling you since November:

The Union is Here to Stay!

The committee joined me at the union hall that Wednesday, all wearing their *No Union Busters* shirts. "What do y'all think?" I asked.

"I'm so excited it feels like I could explode," exclaimed Jeff. "We won! We Won!"

I inquired how people were reacting in the plant. Bill said some of them were still a bit confused. Everyone on both sides was saying the fight was over, but workers were still getting contacted by lawyers to schedule prep meetings.

"There's nothing we can do about that," I replied. "Frankly, it was so sudden that it hardly feels real to me."

"It don't feel real to me either," said the vice president. "It feels kind of empty...."

"Any other intel from inside the plant?"

"Well, a lot of folks are saying that Friday afternoon, Daphne was called up into the front office to meet with Leslie Taylor, and an hour later she came back on the floor with her head down, looking like a whipped dog."

Darnell added Justin had been summoned to a meeting in Calhoun on Wednesday and didn't return until Friday. I thought for a moment and offered my best guess: A senior executive finally took a good look at the Eden situation: someone who didn't usually focus on individual plants, but rather the corporation as a whole. He asked his subordinates why they wanted to stay involved in a labor dispute and trial they couldn't win as negative publicity mounted. He probably told his plant manager to *shut this damn thing down and do it now!*

Darnell asked about Daphne, saying he thought it was up to her whether to withdraw the petition.

"Technically it is. But remember who was backing her in the first place. The truth is, in every other decert I've done, the company got the petitioner to pull the petition once they knew they were whipped. Whatever promises were made to her by management, Daphne doesn't want to lose favor with them now. It will be interesting to see what the company does with her."

CHAPTER 15

Injured Workers

Calvin's grievance meeting had previously been scheduled for the morning of August 3 in the plant conference room. Though not intentionally planned, I welcomed the opportunity to face management across the table several days after their capitulation.

I arrived an hour early to prep with the grievant and committee members. I reviewed the evidence and how our entire case rested on the just cause ban against disparate enforcement of plant rules. The two most meaningless principles in a legal case are *common sense* and *fair*. Familiarity with the underlying logic behind statutes and contract language is essential to providing competent representation. Plant rule enforcement has nothing to do with the fairness of equal treatment. Rather, just cause demands an employer provide the workforce with clear and unambiguous *notice* of what's expected.

An employee who observes a given offense being tolerated for co-workers might assume management isn't serious about enforcing its written policy and act accordingly. The evidence was clear that other employees in Calvin's department hadn't been disciplined for not wearing safety equipment. During the days leading up to the meeting, it appeared as if we might have a viable case. But digging deeper into his file, I learned that following repeat incidents, he'd been personally instructed to never again fail to wear safety glasses. Management had thus met its *notice* requirement in regard to the grievant.

I explained all of this to Calvin and the committee. I never play games with people's expectations. The best I could attempt was to negotiate a *last chance agreement*, if the grievant could act like a gentleman and restrain his temper.

I summoned the company and four members of management sat across from the committee and me: Justin Scarbrough, Leslie Taylor, Elise Griffin and Margie Clemmons. I sensed a well-controlled discomfort and uncertainty on their part. Most of the discussion took place between Leslie and me. She remained her smiling affable self as if the past ten months had been a movie we'd seen on television. Calvin punctuated my well-prepared presentation with an emotional outburst.

Justin took the floor once the grievance had concluded and asked if the union would be open to a state-of-the-business report. I took this as a gesture of his desire to resume a normal relationship, responding we couldn't bargain responsibly without knowing what was happening on their end. Justin proceeded to discuss market conditions for the products manufactured in each of their weaving areas.

"Bottom line: are you in the red or black for 2018?" I asked.

"We're still operating in the red. The rug business continues to decline due to lack of consumer demand and offshore competition. Our wall-to-wall carpets are turning a slight profit and aviation is currently flat."

But there was also positive news. Last month, Mohawk had purchased Godfrey Hearst, a New Zealand plant manufacturing woolen yarn less expensively than Mohawk's current suppliers. The acquisition presented an opportunity to become more cost-competitive with offshore rivals and provided access to rug markets in Australia and New Zealand.

Leslie excused herself for the five-hour drive back to Calhoun, Georgia. "We're going to be dealing with each other going forward on various issues," I said, "so let's exchange cell numbers." I slid business cards across the table to all but Margie. Justin and Leslie readily reciprocated.

"I didn't bring a card with me," said Elise.

"That's OK. Just tell me your cell number and I'll write it down."

She hesitated, looked across at her superiors who remained expressionless, and provided the information. I stood up and walked around the table shaking hands. Margie Clemmons was sitting the farthest from me. She was obliged to rise and extend her hand, which I held firmly for a few seconds, staring calmly into her eyes. She had an expression of distaste as if being forced to handle a dangerous reptile.

I clustered with committee members in the reception room to review the session. Another piece of the puzzle had been revealed. Mohawk had just spent a fortune on a new plant to service ours, making a huge commitment to our end of the business. It didn't make sense to invest that sort of money and then continue having the mill destabilized by a losing fight.

I scheduled a committee meeting for the following week and encountered Tim and Brenna upon entering the union hall, still prepping witnesses for the unlikely event of a trial. I thanked them for their efforts and how seriously they'd taken our case.

"It looks like carpet-bombing the plant with your subpoenas worked after all. It scared the shit out of everyone ... probably the company in particular. I think the gravity of all this might have finally hit home with the right people."

The committee remained jubilant as they took their usual seats around our table-array. I discussed the Board's settlement terms offered to the company.

"Justin having to get up in front of all the people in meetings, just like he did during their captive audiences in October, and admit what the company did.... I really like that part," said Bill. "It will mean a whole lot more than a bunch of damn postings."

On Saturday, August 11, Local 294-T held a victory picnic at Freedom Park in Eden. Committee members worked the grills and some of the women had prepared side dishes. Patricia brought a Crock-Pot filled with her home-style recipe for baked beans. The bright Carolina sun was interrupted by summer showers but folks waited them out under the shelter. I came expecting to just relax and enjoy myself but encountered union members with problems to discuss.

During mid-afternoon, a woman appearing in her late thirties arrived with two teenage sons, walking toward an unoccupied corner table in the rear. She was beautiful in a unique, somewhat offbeat way, wearing a low-cut summer dress with a floral design. *Don't even think about it,* I told myself while approaching to introduce myself.

She shook my hand and invited me to sit. Her name was Jessie Dotson. I'd never encountered her while touring the plant because she'd been cloistered in a small office on *light duty* due to a shoulder injury sustained at work. I requested details and asked if she had a lawyer.

Jessie worked as a *creel hand,* supplying yarn to carpet-weaving looms. The problem with her shoulder had slowly evolved over time from occasional discomfort to severe pain and lack of mobility. It was the most common form of injury found in textile mills: ergonomic. The repetitive motion inherent in many jobs gradually wears down a person's joints until they become disabled, impacting wrists, elbows, shoulders, knees and backs. Like other on-the-job injuries, this is covered by workers compensation.

Workers comp is an insurance policy similar to automobile insurance. Companies are required to be insured and premiums rise with each successful claim. Mohawk is insured by Liberty Mutual. When multiplied against the number of workers in a national corporation, rising premiums result in serious red ink on balance sheets. Employers are therefore ruthless in seeking to minimize exposure. Ergonomic injuries are often discredited as having preexisted employment or originated at home. When a doctor authenticates an injury as job related, management reduces liability by feigning concern for the employee, while failing to inform them of rights guaranteed by workers comp statutes.

Jessie had obtained sufficient medical documentation. Mohawk was paying her doctor bills and providing work in an office with minimal assignments. I asked if she'd filed a workers comp claim and was told Elise hadn't offered one.

"The company never does," I told her. "They're not doing you any favors. If they put you on workers comp leave, the insurance company would have to pay two-thirds of your wages. They'd rather pay you full salary for doing nothing than have their insurance rating lowered. Management acts like your best friend, covering the deductibles in your medical insurance. But your case sounds like you're probably entitled to big money they'd rather you not know about."

"Elise called me into her office and told me she'd contacted my doctor and he said I could go back to work. That's not what it says on the form I got from my doctor and I told her so."

"Good for you for sticking up for yourself," I told her, "but let me explain your rights and what you should do. Take someone from the committee with you up to the office and request a workers comp claim form. Elise is required by law to give you one."

Filing a workers comp claim evokes a menu of entitlements that can change an injured worker's life, but are costly to employers. Every body part has been assigned a monetary value. Following medical treatment and rehab, employees are given a disability rating. If an index finger is fully lost, the person gets its full value. If impaired but still functional, she gets the amount specified by her partial disability rating.

"It's kind of grisly," I told Jessie, "but we're talking about some serious money."

Having a claim on file also means if an employee returns to work feeling better, but years later the injury resurfaces, the company's insurance remains liable, even if the person is working elsewhere. The North Carolina Industrial Commission enforces regulations and adjudicates disputes in our state. The process of negotiating settlements with insurance companies or litigating before the Commission is complicated and requires an attorney specializing in this area. I offered Jessie the phone number of Hank Patterson, with whom I'd worked throughout my career.

"I thought of doing all that," she said, "but then a woman I work with told me if I did, I'd have a bullseye painted on my back. I can't afford to lose my job."

I explained that retaliation for exercising workers comp rights was illegal. It might happen in nonunion plants but not here. She'd suffered a lot from doing her job and was legally entitled to compensation.

"Hey, Ma," her eldest son interjected. "Maybe they'll end up paying you a thousand dollars!"

"I can't make any promises," I said, "but it will probably be a hell of a lot more than that."

Evening was upon us and the crowd thinned. As Patricia and I prepared to leave, Thomas handed me a bag filled with the largest slicing tomatoes I'd ever seen, then followed us to the car carrying an enormous watermelon.

On Monday morning, Mohawk Industries, through its attorney, executed a Settlement Agreement with the National Labor Relations Board. The employer would be required to post notices throughout the plant and on all TV monitors for sixty days. The posting contained fourteen statements beginning with WE WILL NOT, each addressing an allegation in the Complaint:

WE WILL NOT ask you to sign a petition to remove the Union as your bargaining representative.

The Admission and Reading of Notice clauses had been deleted. Tim's response was, "We still have the default language." He referred to a section stating if the employer reneged on the settlement, either by failing to comply with posting or engaging in repeat violations, it would be deemed an admission of guilt not subject to appeal.

That was it: game over. The corporation's penalty for having engaged in a conspiracy to deprive workers of their rights under federal law would be to post an embarrassing notice. Mohawk would have to continue bargaining with the union and Fredrick didn't get to chalk one up in his win column. For his part-time machinations, the attorney was probably paid several times more than the executive board's combined yearly earnings.

Chapter 15. Injured Workers

On August 15, Jeff and I toured the plant as conquering heroes. I was overwhelmed by the outpouring of gratitude. Our management chaperones lagged twenty yards behind while we chose the route. In the Mending Department we came upon Ray Santos, conversing with an anti-union employee. I walked directly toward him, extending my hand and making eye contact, asking, "How are you today, Ray?" He continued grinning while I held onto his hand and squeezed harder than necessary.

I met with the committee afterward to explain the company's final Settlement Agreement. "That ain't right," said Bill. It was the most upset I'd ever seen him at a meeting. "They need to admit what they done and get up in front of the people and say it. That's the least we can expect after all they tried to get away with."

"Why'd you let them take that part out?" asked Darnell. "I can't go along with that. You should have at least brought it to the committee before you agreed."

I explained we didn't have any say in the matter. Settlement negotiations are between the Board and employer. The union isn't involved. I suggested looking at the big picture. We won. Our mission was to expose a corrupt scheme and save the union. We did that in triplicate. There was no need to get hung up on payback. We could spread the message any way we wanted.

Darnell said he now understood the union's position but wanted to know why Tim let them off so easily, after seeming to really believe in our case.

I expressed doubt he even had a choice. The Board had two attorneys working full-time prepping for a trial that one way or the other wasn't going to happen. Someone higher-up probably told him to wrap this and placed other cases on his desk. The same thing happens in criminal court: prosecutors make deals to clear their calendar.

"There's rumors going around the plant about Daphne," said Jeff. "People been telling me she's posting things on Facebook bashing both the union and the company. Someone said she posted a picture of herself with her middle finger out and the words said 'F* the union and F* the company.'"

"Can you send me a copy of that? I'd love to see it."

"I tried looking for it, but Facebook must have taken it down."

The next morning I called Hank Patterson to brief him on Jessie's situation, suggesting if he didn't hear from her, to reach out on his end.

I then prepared a leaflet with a positive spin on the final outcome of our ten-month campaign:

Part Two—The Case Unfolds

MOHAWK SIGNS SETTLEMENT WITH NLRB

Confronted by overwhelming evidence and a trial they couldn't win, Mohawk signed a settlement agreement with the NLRB.

In a couple of weeks, the company will post notices on all bulletin boards and TV monitors, addressing the violations cited by the government. United States attorneys will *re-open the case and prosecute Mohawk if it repeats the violations.*

Compliance Officer Jenny Dunn was assigned by Region 10 to close out the case. The postings were being printed on an official NLRB template, and also needed to be translated into Spanish. Preparation was expected to take at least two weeks.

I wrote Tim to ask how long the default language in Mohawk's Settlement would remain enforceable and he responded:

> There is no sunset provision so, technically, the default language remains in effect in perpetuity. That being said, the more time that passes from the signing of the agreement, I imagine, the less likely it would be that the GC would seek enforcement.

On August 23, the Office of the NLRB's General Counsel in Washington rejected Fredrick's appeal of the union's Settlement Agreement.

"That's the good news," I told the committee. "But it means we're going to have to put up our own posting soon. But the appeal delayed things to the point it will probably coincide with the company's posting. Theirs is so much more serious that ours will probably get lost in the shuffle."

Darnell asked if the various postings would be on TV monitors. I replied that Mohawk's would, but we only had to hang ours on the four union bulletin boards.

I passed out copies of Mohawk's posting and then ours, giving the committee a few minutes to read. Bill held up the union's notice. "This is just a bunch of piddly shit. I ain't worried about it. The important thing is, we won."

PART THREE

Aftermath

The object of war is always peace.—Sun Tzu, *The Art of War*

CHAPTER 16

Compliance Period

Workers United Local 294-T and management at the Mohawk facility in Eden entered into a phase analogous to the Marshall Plan after World War II. Peace doesn't begin the day fighting ends, and the troops don't immediately go home. Cooperation is more complicated and far less glamorous than battle. We needed to forge a new and sustainable balance of power. It would require finding ways to support the plant becoming profitable without sacrificing the rights of our members.

As the parties eased back into a normal collective bargaining process, the committee experienced a difficult transition. A couple of the guys had lived their entire lives secretly yearning to become involved in a major labor dispute. Triumph is more seductive and intoxicating than any drug. I began a slow process of helping them unwind and realize that rubbing management's nose in their defeat would be of no service to our members.

Anthony Coles announced his retirement and Harris Raynor consolidated the Carolinas/Virginia District with the adjoining Mid-South District under the leadership of its manager Niecy Brown. I entered the union hall one afternoon and a distraught Taina informed me the building had been sold. It would remain ours to use for several weeks until the sale closed. I felt bad for Taina who was about to be laid off, but grateful the old building had been there for us throughout the campaign.

On August 29, we held our last shift meetings at the labor movement's historic outpost. Turnout was light, as workers already knew they'd finally learned the whole truth. I used the committee meeting that followed to discuss how we could reopen channels of diplomacy with management from a new position of power. I'd seen too many locals where legitimate issues went unresolved for years as the parties engaged in endless squabbling while the caseload mounted.

"I got no use for these people, but I know I've got to deal with them as mill chair to help our people," said Darnell. "But when I do, I'm gonna be getting in their face and giving them a hard time. That's just part of what I do."

I let it go, believing he was just blowing off steam and talking tough. Jeff showed us one of Daphne's Facebook posts on his phone:

Come to the UNION Meeting!!!! They are going to tell you the real truth!!! I sure hope they didn't get that information from my "closest confident" ... we all know I'm sitting pretty in that safety position that's higher than management.

From the NLRB's perspective, we'd entered into the Compliance Period. Jenny Dunn requested a list of all locations the company utilized to post hard-copy notices and all TV monitors. On September 5, both parties began their sixty-day posting period. Mohawk hung its lengthy statement on bulletin boards and next to time clocks in fifteen areas. The electronic version appeared in a half-dozen breakrooms and all department television screens. Workers clustered around, trying to make sense of it. The union's posting captured little attention. People seldom bothered with our bulletin boards, when so much information was available in leaflets. I prepared a new handout:

There are several important differences between the NLRB settlements signed by Mohawk and the union, including:

- A complaint was not issued against the union.
- The union's settlement contains this clause:

NON-ADMISSION CLAUSE—By entering into this Settlement Agreement, the Charged Party does not admit that it has violated the National Labor Relations Act.

- Mohawk's settlement does not contain a Non-Admission Clause.

The committee remained vigilant of Mohawk's compliance. Jeff took photographs of printed notices positioned too high or low for easy reading and monitor postings with small print changing frames too quickly. Mike sent them to Jenny Dunn, who had management make the necessary adjustments. Fredrick continued to complain about my leaflets to the Board but no one was interested.

Jeff, Darnell and I gave a victory presentation at the District Conference in Charlotte during the second weekend in September. In my mind, this marked the campaign's finale.

Justin called on Monday morning to discuss corporate safety programs he'd been instructed to implement at the Eden facility. Workers would be required to wear orange shirts or vests to increase their visibility to forklift drivers. Each person would be issued two T-shirts bearing the

Mohawk emblem and one vest. A *Neighborhood Watch* program would be started, encouraging employees to report safety hazards and unsafe conduct by co-workers. I told him both initiatives raised serious concerns and we needed to schedule a meeting. The inevitable onslaught of unexpected local issues had begun.

That afternoon, I received an email from Ed Cheroff, Mohawk's long-standing labor attorney, with whom Harris had a relationship. He asked to schedule a phone call to "touch base" regarding these matters. Two days later, we introduced ourselves over the phone. Ed had resumed his role as Mohawk's outside counsel for labor relations. I asked if Fredrick was still involved behind the scenes and he professed no knowledge. The lawyer requested my objections to the safety programs so he could explain them to his client.

Discussions of this nature are often fruitful and result in expedited settlements. Seasoned labor attorneys speak the same language as union reps and can sometimes serve as better intermediaries with corporate decision makers than local management. I always first seek employee input and make it clear any deals will have to be negotiated across the table with local officers present. The union's goal was no longer ensnaring management in cumbersome litigation but rather resolving issues quickly to the benefit of our members.

I conveyed my understanding that plant managers were under pressure to adopt corporate programs at their location. Executives expect conformity at all facilities but that doesn't supersede a union contract. Many collective bargaining agreements provide employer discretion to implement rules, but the union can file grievances if policies are considered *unreasonable*. Our contract lacked such a clause, making the proposed changes *mandatory subjects of bargaining*. The NLRB has a list of *mandatory subjects* that includes safety.

Ed interjected and we had a polite debate for ten minutes as to whether the employer was required to bargain in this instance. "We could both spend a month writing briefs on this subject," said the attorney. "For now, let's just say we disagree and our positions have been duly noted."

This matter wasn't going to be resolved over the phone and I began to address the corporate safety programs, arguing they had no relevance at the Karastan rug mill: a stand-alone facility owned by a company primarily in the business of tile and wooden floor coverings. "I've toured the plant numerous times. The aisles are so wide and well-lit that a forklift driver would have to be aiming at a co-worker to hit him."

Employees objected to the notion of *being dressed like a pumpkin* every day at work. "How would you like it if every day you had to wear an orange suit to work?" I asked the attorney.

"Our only interest is the safety of our employees," he responded as if none of the union's issues had been raised. I understood he was simply maintaining his client's position and would convey our concerns to the right people. My attention turned to Neighborhood Watch. I supported the concept of employees reporting safety hazards on the shop floor but took issue regarding them informing management of infractions by co-workers.

I followed up with Mike after the conversation. We agreed that the shirts were arguably a mandatory subject of bargaining, but not the reporting policy as it would only be voluntary.

The committee and I met with management the following afternoon to discuss changes in medical insurance prior to the annual open enrollment period. It's become customary for union plants within predominantly nonunion companies to be covered by corporate benefit plans, rather than negotiate separate policies. The massive premium discounts offered by providers on a national basis far outweigh anything that could be negotiated locally.

The committee and I remained in the conference room once the brief benefits meeting adjourned. The timing was fortunate. We no longer had access to a union hall and there was much to discuss.

"I don't like Justin and the company lawyer coming to you directly about the orange shirts," said Darnell. "They should have come to me as the mill chair."

I explained this was how business was done in the real world. "Unlike some union reps, I'm not going to bullshit you about it. I'll never make a deal behind your back and the only suggestions I make will be based on your input. But our members need to see results now that we won, and I'll do whatever it takes to get them."

"Let's talk about the damn shirts so we can all get the hell out of here," suggested Bill.

I reviewed my discussion with Ed and requested input to solidify our position before scheduling a meeting with Justin. Word was already out on the floor, courtesy of supervisors with big mouths. Workers were not only upset by the orange dress code but concerned about receiving only two shirts and a vest.

"How the hell am I supposed to come to work every day with only the same two shirts?" asked Bill. "Either I start to smell or have to stand over the sink washing one out every evening." He suggested that if all else failed, we should request five shirts and a choice of orange or lime green (also a standard visibility color).

"I'm not going along with any of this," said Darnell. "This is a mandatory subject of bargaining and they can't do it if we say no."

I offered a broader view. While the NLRB requires employers to bargain with unions, if *impasse* is reached after discussion has been exhausted, management can implement its final offer. This usually doesn't pose a serious threat during contract negotiations. With numerous proposals on the table, a skilled union rep can keep the ball in the air indefinitely. But here, there was only one simple issue at play. Absent compromise, we'd end up with the same two orange shirts as other Mohawk plants, and workers would blame us.

Thomas was offended by having to wear the Mohawk logo to work. They'd just blown out all the stops trying to destroy us, and now expected us to proudly display their emblem. We agreed to propose a choice of shirts, either plain or bearing the Karastan logo.

Committee members were vehemently opposed to Neighborhood Watch, fearing safety violations reported by co-workers would lead to discipline. Our job was to represent disciplined employees, not support policies resulting in additional write-ups.

"I ain't no rat," said Bill. "If this is gonna be voluntary, we should tell everyone to stay away from it."

I agreed with him in principle. Where I came from in New York, there was nothing lower than a snitch. I'd raised my daughter in the ethic of being *stand up*. If she had problems with another student, I taught her to settle it herself and never involve the teacher.

I told committee members it was time to schedule a formal meeting with Justin. We discussed possible locations for future union meetings but thus far nothing had presented itself.

Leslie Taylor emailed Calvin's third step answer. As expected, the grievance was denied based on his cumulative history of rule violations. I called to let her know off-the-record that the union wouldn't be filing for arbitration, preferring to save my credibility and clout for better cases.

Many workers believe arbitration is simply another step in the grievance procedure: an informal hour involving an outside party. It's actually a trial, held pursuant to contract language, rather than state or federal law. A hearing usually lasts a full day as motions are argued and witnesses testify under oath. Briefs are filed and a decision rendered within thirty days. Litigants split the cost. Many arbitrators charge well over $1000 per day (including post-hearing review of evidence and preparing the lengthy *award*). The process forces both sides to get real during the endgame. Neither wants to make the considerable investment of time and resources in a lost cause.

Jeff called with surprise news regarding a meeting space. The Eden Public Library had made its conference rooms available to us free of charge.

While management focused on health and safety from the perspective of corporate compliance, I chose to focus on it by educating workers about their rights. My first leaflet on the subject began with the heading **If You Get Injured at Work**. I provided the same information given to Jessie Dotson at the picnic and concluded by saying:

> Talk to a workers comp lawyer. Don't go it alone. Companies get workers comp coverage through an insurance company. The insurance turns down most claims, because they don't want to pay. A good lawyer makes them pay.
>
> Workers comp lawyers are standing by to give free consultations to members.

CHAPTER 17

The Tornado

I drove down Hwy. 158 toward Eden on September 25 for a *Labor Management Meeting* to address safety policies. I thought to myself: *Three months ago, I was preparing witnesses for trial. Now I'm about to have a serious discussion about orange shirts.* The committee joined me in the plant conference room at 1 p.m. We agreed that given our vulnerability to impasse, the shirts were inevitable, but we were in a position to push our proposals. Management didn't want us putting out leaflets opposing the program.

I invited management into the room and Justin took his customary seat at the head of the table. I sat immediately to his left, opposite Elise. Darnell was in the chair next to me and Thomas was several seats down. Bill sat at the far end facing Justin, while Jeff and Tonya (the union's recording secretary) found seats on the other side. I came to realize this would be the standard formation.

Justin began by stating for-the-record the company didn't consider corporate safety programs a mandatory subject of bargaining but was willing to discuss the issues in good faith. There had been a number of changes at other Mohawk facilities put on hold at the Karastan plant during the conflict, and it was now time to address them. I responded that while the union maintained its position that this was a bargaining session, it could remain an academic disagreement if we reached accommodation.

I presented my ground rules for meetings: When someone has the floor they don't get cut off. If a person disagrees, they wait until remarks are finished. I don't tolerate unprofessional conduct from either side. Though a rhetorical question, I asked Justin to explain his reasons for wanting to implement the new safety policies. Following his expected response about how deeply Mohawk cared about employee wellbeing, I suggested we cut to the chase.

I noted we both worked for chain-of-command organizations and understood the pressure he was under regarding corporate conformity.

That was the underlying reason we were sitting at the table. I asked for his response to my position that the new dress code was unnecessary at our plant.

Justin described a significant increase of on-the-job injuries throughout Mohawk. After an employee was seriously injured when hit by a forklift, the company had developed programs to address the problem.

"Thank you," I said. "So this is a workers comp issue." I acknowledged this represented a major cost item, but again questioned how it related to our mill. I'd reviewed the *OSHA 400 logs* (accident and injury reports) and there had been relatively few injuries during the past three years, mostly ergonomic in nature. I asked when there had last been a forklift related injury.

Justin honestly replied, "Not since I've been here."

A good bargaining position had been established and I presented our proposals. Safety equipment was the employer's responsibility and as such, workers should be given a sufficient number of shirts. Forcing employees to purchase additional shirts would represent a unilateral change in *economic terms and conditions.*

"This is a touchy subject," I said, "but many workers are still deeply upset by Mohawk's actions during the decert, and don't want to wear their logo. But everyone's proud of the Karastan brand and the craftsmanship they contribute. Offer a choice of logos and this will go down a lot smoother."

Justin said he'd have to discuss our proposals with his superiors and schedule a follow-up meeting. This was to be expected since we were suggesting improvements to a corporate program that wouldn't be offered in dozens of other plants.

The more emotional topic was next on the agenda. Justin described the Neighborhood Watch Program in detail. Workers would be encouraged to report structural and machine hazards to management, along with unsafe actions by fellow employees. The offender's name would be kept out of the report. Management was simply seeking opportunities to raise employee awareness.

"Do you mind if I say something?" Bill asked and I nodded. "Some of these jobs only have two or three people per shift. You know supervisors are going to follow up on a report by coming into the work area, finding out who did what and then writing them up."

"Information provided by employees under Neighborhood Watch will not result in discipline," said Justin. "You have my word."

"Would you be willing to put that in writing?" I asked.

Chapter 17. The Tornado

Justin agreed and I offered to prepare a *memorandum of agreement* (MOA).

I caucused with the committee for awhile and as I left the conference room, Justin motioned me into his office. "We've got an awkward situation, perhaps you could help us with," he said. The mill was in the process of being audited for quality certification now essential for future airline business. This has become common practice in many industries and plants rise or fall based on qualifying. (The most well-known certification program is ISO 9000.) Employee conduct is one of many areas evaluated.

Darnell had refused to sign a document stating he'd received and understood recent training associated with certification. Justin said if this was discovered during an audit of company records by airline representatives, it would compromise certification. I promised to address his concern at our next committee meeting.

I met Niecy Brown for dinner when she was in the area a few days later, to update the Carolinas/Virginia District's new manager. We first met in 1988 when she was union president at Phoenix Glove in Andrews, South Carolina, where I was running a campaign at Anthony's local. It was remarkable that two factory workers from a small southern backwater with one traffic light had risen to become union directors.

Niecy is the crème de la crème of organizers, having spent many years in the field directing campaigns. She's a beautiful woman whose age is hard to guess; sweet-natured with a big heart, but tough as nails when necessary. During the recent district merger, Niecy became responsible for locals in seven states. She lived and worked out of her car but the wear and tear never showed on her face or in how she treated others.

I discussed our progress at repairing the bargaining relationship and the tensions within the committee as the process normalized. Our biggest challenge would be membership building and we'd remain vulnerable unless this could be achieved. The decert had followed years of complacency as union reps became too comfortable with what appeared to be a stable situation, neglecting to encourage workers to sign union cards. The opportunity had been overlooked during the mass hiring of 2016. Enjoying the benefits of representation without paying dues had gradually become an established part of the culture.

We were further hampered by contract language. Most of our plants now had agreements allowing free access to union reps, unaccompanied by management. We also had an hour of union orientation for new hires, paid for by the employer. It was comparatively easy to sign cards under these circumstances. But the draconian language in the Mohawk contract provided for neither. Our only option was the old-school approach: making *house calls.*

The next morning I contacted the office manager in Atlanta and asked her to prepare *house call sheets*, each listing the name, address, job, shift and demographics of a nonmember. This information is provided by management in quarterly seniority lists. The sheets offer organizers a snapshot of whom to expect when the next door opens.

October 11 was an unseasonably cool day with moderate rainfall. The National Weather Service believed this to be the outer fringe of hurricane Michael, on a trajectory bypassing central North Carolina. I headed toward Eden for another plant visit.

Jeff and I were accompanied by two members of midlevel management. After visiting the larger departments, Jeff led us through Rug Fabrication and Finishing. Workers stood at large worktables, applying the final touches to rugs before they were stockpiled as inventory. Ray Santos was nowhere to be seen and Jeff said he'd disappeared several weeks ago.

We descended two winding flights of cement stairs to visit the Dye House, where color was applied to raw yarn before being sent to Yarn Prep. I noticed an enormous cauldron of steaming water and questioned its purpose. The department head explained certain types of yarn required washing prior to dying.

"Do you ever throw a chicken in there for lunch?" I asked and he laughed.

As we headed back to the front office, I looked out a window, observing heavy rainfall and strong winds. Loudspeakers suddenly announced a tornado warning, instructing everyone to take shelter in a room at the building's lowest level. Jeff and I soon stood within a mixed assembly of workers, management and visitors. I was prepared to leave and take my chances but understood the company's liability concerns.

A siren ended the official warning and I walked through the parking lot, drenched in downpour and buffeted by strong winds. Jeff had offered to let me wait out the storm at his house but I wanted to get home, trusting in my ability to drive through anything. As Hwy. 14 narrowed into 158, the rain and wind gathered intensity.

I kept my speed around forty until approaching a large tree fallen across the road, leaving just enough space to get around with two wheels on someone's lawn. A couple of minutes later there was another uprooted tree, leaving part of the opposing lane free. It became increasingly difficult to hold my car steady in the gale, as I zigzagged my way through trees now littering the pavement every hundred yards.

A power line hovered several feet above the road. I slowed to a crawl, assessing passability and feeling reasonably confident the low design of my Charger could make it. I slowly passed with an inch to spare and continued through the carnage for another half-hour. It was obvious from woodland on both sides that tornadoes had touched down. It felt like driving through the apocalypse. Eventually I came to an ancient tree fully blocking the road. Repair crews estimated its removal would take several hours and directed me toward a complicated series of detours. Patricia called to say our power had gone out.

I continued through a confusing sequence of two-lane roads, doing my best to remember the instructions, periodically changed by work crews dealing with new disasters. Four hours later I pulled into a convenience store twenty miles from home to pick up bottled water for the power outage. I returned to my car carrying an armful of gallon jugs, popped the trunk and placed them inside. As I withdrew my hands, a violent gust of wind slammed the trunk shut with the force of a bullet, nicking two fingers on my right hand. Had I been one second later, my guitar playing days would have been over.

The remaining half-hour was uneventful as the rain and wind gradually subsided. Patricia stood near my parking spot, dressed in her rain gear, saying she had something major to report. We had a large cedar tree growing directly alongside our house. It had sprouted many years ago and though it defied logical precautions, we fell in love with the sapling and couldn't bring ourselves to remove it. A dying tree from the grove in front had blown over, headed directly for the roof above my office. The cedar we'd spared had caught the falling tree and tossed it harmlessly out of the way.

CHAPTER 18

House Calls

I joined Niecy, Bill and Jeff for dinner on Friday, October 19, to prepare for a weekend of house calls. The director had surprised me by volunteering to help, on what might have been a rare two days off. Workers United could no longer afford an organizing staff and SEIU had no one available. The best house call teams consist of an experienced staff member supported by a worker sharing their personal experiences.

Bill met me in front of the Hampton Inn at 9 a.m. on a cold, dreary morning. He took the passenger seat in my car and we set the GPS for our first address. We headed down Hwy. 14 until directed to turn right, commencing what would be my guided tour of Eden: a primarily residential community comprised of working-class neighborhoods dotted with churches, closed factories, and the occasional small business.

"Your destination is on the right," said the alien who speaks through my phone. We knocked but no one was home. We returned to the car through a light drizzle and Bill chose our next destination. An old woman opened the door and said we had the wrong address. We marked the sheet accordingly and proceeded. I suggested visiting Annie, noting she'd make an incredible shop steward if persuaded to sign a card. Bill knew where she lived and a few minutes later we were knocking on the door of her trailer. We heard sounds from within but no one came to the door.

"She must have seen us through the window," said Bill, "and don't want no part of the union today."

Disappointed, I asked him to pick another name. We entered a parking lot with two-story apartment buildings and spent ten minutes finding the right door. A woman answered, telling us the man we were seeking had recently moved, but she was able to provide his new address. We drove several miles to learn he hadn't stayed there very long.

We finally found a young black woman who actually worked at the mill. She invited us into her modest living room and after an hour of polite conversation told us she'd have to "think about" joining. I suggested we regroup over lunch at Subway. After finishing his sandwich, Bill spent a half-hour sorting through the sheets, selecting our next visits.

My partner knew the address of another nonmember who'd been a willing participant in the NLRB case. We headed through a labyrinth of curving two-lane roads that must have evolved from centuries-old horse trails. There was no apparent grid or evidence of civic planning. Bill offered descriptions and history of various neighborhoods as we drove. The person we sought wasn't home.

The next two addresses were wrong. I called Niecy and learned her team was having a similar experience. We agreed to wrap the misadventure until I could get to the bottom of why the company had provided so much incorrect information.

I called Elise on Monday and was told employees were encouraged to update addresses via the company website, but it wasn't enforced. Bill agreed this was true. I emailed the HR director requesting a list of recent hires with addresses included.

I joined committee members at the Eden Public Library on November 13. We were ushered into the Local History Room and took seats around a large conference table surrounded by bookshelves on all sides. The shelf behind me contained several dozen thick volumes, documenting every North Carolina soldier who'd served during the Civil War. The front wall displayed pictures of previous governors.

The committee seemed in good spirits as we prepared for our follow-up meeting with Justin regarding safety initiatives, scheduled for two days later. I distributed copies of the MOA emailed to the plant manager regarding Neighborhood Watch:

> Both parties hereby agree that information provided to management pursuant to the Neighborhood Watch Program is for the purpose of identifying and correcting safety hazards, and will not result in the discipline of bargaining unit employees.

Darnell said word was out on the floor regarding the orange shirts and he was being overwhelmed with questions, responding only that negotiations were still in progress.

Committee members began addressing several new issues. Management had posted updated seniority lists in each department. Aviation employees were in an uproar regarding two workers hired in 2016 from the closed Landrum facility: anti-union petitioner Mia Linares and her husband, Joseph. The list indicated they'd been allowed to keep their company seniority, violating the contract and placing them over employees with greater plant seniority in the event of a layoff.

A worker named Reggie Anderson had been terminated for sexual harassment, allegedly using his phone to photograph his penis and then showing it to a female employee. Darnell pointed out it wasn't the first time committee members had heard complaints from women about this married employee.

"This is one of the most bizarre cases I've ever heard of," I said but promised to make the usual request for the company's evidence.

Bill raised another concern from Aviation workers. A lead person named Christine had been working sixty to seventy hours per week while bargaining unit employees in that department were on *short time*. Similar to most union contracts, there was a strict prohibition against management or other nonbargaining personnel performing duties that deprived hourly workers of earning potential. The vice president had requested Christine's Kronos records to investigate the concern but Elise had been unresponsive. Darnell discussed employee complaints about one of the breakrooms being infested with roaches. Management at other Mohawk facilities would have lacked accountability and enjoyed sole discretion regarding all of these issues.

I eased my way into discussing the quality certification mentioned by Justin, careful not to come across as taking the plant manager's side in an issue involving the mill chair. I addressed the whole committee, explaining how qualification would be essential to the plant's future and ensuring our members' job security.

"I refused to sign that paper they gave me," said Darnell. "The company don't tell me when to sign my name."

I told him we couldn't represent people that didn't have jobs and urged him to reconsider.

Two days later at 1 p.m. we took our usual seats around the company conference table, and I asked Justin for a state-of-the business update. Aviation was in fact running on short time while certain looms in the main Weave Room were operating six to seven days per week. This is not uncommon in market-driven textile operations, resulting in some employees getting worked to death while others barely pay their bills. Management was optimistic regarding new products being introduced in their residential carpet line. Mohawk's stock price had plummeted during the past several months from $280 to $125 per share. Paul DeCock had taken over as the company's President of Flooring North America. He was introducing new budgeting procedures and measures for optimizing each plant.

"Where do we stand on shirts?" I asked.

Justin had been authorized to accept all of our proposals. Each employee would be issued five shirts and a vest; allowed to choose between orange or lime green from a selection of unmarked apparel, or items bearing either the Mohawk or Karastan insignia. He noticed Darnell wearing his own orange shirt displaying the Workers United logo and acknowledged that as an alternative. Following further discussion, it was agreed the brightly colored clothing wouldn't become mandatory until January 1, with a thirty-day grace period before discipline was issued.

"We appreciate your flexibility," I said. "When will I receive the signed MOA on Neighborhood Watch?"

"I've got no problems with your language," Justin replied. "But I've got to run it by our lawyers."

I presented issues raised at our recent committee meeting. Justin promised to expedite the outstanding information requests and provide documents regarding the transfer of Landrum employees to our facility. We all shook hands and the committee remained with me after management left. "That went fairly well," Darnell acknowledged.

"That's the purpose of building a relationship. Things don't get worked out that easily when both sides are always picking at each other."

The productive meeting with Justin proved to be my final visit to Eden during 2018, but I continued to engage the local and management from home. I wrote the next in my series of educational leaflets, this time addressing FMLA:

> **Intermittent Leave**—If you or a dependent have an ongoing health problem that causes you to miss work only when it flares up, you're probably covered. Examples include migraine headaches, anxiety disorder, diabetes, and many others.
>
> - You'll need to get a form from HR, and take it to your doctor.
> - Once you get certified, *qualifying absences can't be held against you.*
> - If you've been written-up for what should have been FMLA, *the warnings can probably be removed once you get certified*—if someone in management knew of your condition, but didn't inform you of your rights.
> - This is *enforced by federal law through the Department of Labor.*

As promised, I filed a third step grievance on behalf of Reggie Anderson, accompanied by the standard information request. While his claim of innocence regarding sexual impropriety wasn't credible even to the committee, we would remain his advocate until documentation shut us down. There are times when due process errors by management allow us to enforce just cause on behalf of employees who are guilty as sin. I have no qualms about this. Corporations, represented by a room full of high-priced lawyers and executives, are routinely exonerated for infractions far worse than any worker could commit. The only person a terminated employee has in his corner is me.

CHAPTER 19

Shop Floor Confrontation

Bill and I met in front of the Eden Library on Friday morning, January 4, the final weekday of the plant's holiday shutdown. We sat in the conference room for half an hour while Bill shuffled through house call sheets to organize our itinerary.

We headed down Hwy. 14 on a cold but sunny day, passing our old union hall on the right. We focused on workers hired two or three years before, realizing they'd probably never been spoken to about the union, and were less likely to have moved since putting their address on a job application. Curious and friendly people invited us in and appeared open-minded as we described how the union was responsible for the wages and working conditions that first attracted them to the mill. But eyes grew wide and nervous when I finally put a membership card in someone's hand. The best response we could get was a promise to *think about it.*

"People act like we're asking them to join a secret cult where we drink goat blood under the full moon each month," I remarked to Bill as we left the home of a young lady who'd seemed a promising candidate. It was astonishing that in 2019, workers in an eighty-year-old local considered the union such an ominous mystery.

We had a friendly but unproductive discussion standing outside the door of a maintenance worker. He'd recently applied for the position of safety coordinator but wasn't optimistic. Rumors were circulating that the hiring process was for appearances only and Daphne Little would ultimately get the job.

After lunch we entered the parking lot of a rundown brick building with one-story apartments and knocked on a door. A pleasant young black man in his early twenties invited us in and began attentively listening as we stood in the kitchen. A short burly man with disheveled hair, looking much like Fred Sanford but only meaner, burst into the room.

"What the hell are you doing in here talking to my son?" he demanded. "Get out of my house now!"

Bill calmly explained we were from the union over at the Mohawk plant and had some important information to share.

"I don't work there anymore," said the young man.

"How do you know that?" his father roared. He again demanded we leave.

As we walked back to my car, I remarked, "That was one of the strangest conversations I've ever heard. The kid says he don't work at the plant anymore and his father asks *how he knows.*"

Bill observed how the older man came across like he'd been in prison at some point in his life. "Look at it this way," he said. "Two white guys in leather jackets knocking on doors in this neighborhood. He probably thought we were the police."

At 4 p.m. we called on Elma Howard, one of our key witnesses who'd corroborated Annie Southerland. She greeted us with a smile and we spoke for forty-five minutes standing on the wooden deck in back of an attractive middle class home. She was delighted to have helped the union survive and listened while we explained why people needed to translate their support into membership if we were going to endure. But when Bill finally handed her a card we saw the familiar horrified look in her eyes. As darkness fell, I told Bill this had been the only time I'd house-called for two days without signing a card.

On Monday morning, Elise emailed the bargaining history regarding the transfer of Landrum employees to Eden. During 2015, corporate management had debated whether to close the Landrum or Eden mills, so certain operations could be consolidated within the remaining facility. As a result, the Karastan Aviation Department was expanded, leaving the company desperate to hire experienced carpet weavers and loom mechanics. On October 21, 2015, the union agreed to incentivize skilled Landrum employees to relocate by allowing them to carry company seniority into our plant. A list of eligible candidates was prepared. All other transfers from the nonunion plant would begin as new hires but keep their accrued vacation benefits.

A year later, Darnell filed a grievance because though not on the list, Mia and her husband were allowed to transfer their Landrum seniority to Karastan, violating the agreement and potentially disadvantaging long-term employees. On February 22, 2017, Anthony signed an agreement withdrawing the grievance in exchange for management rehiring two terminated workers.

I called Justin and he privately admitted that in hindsight, the 2017 settlement didn't seem fair to senior workers. Aware of employee sentiment generated by the updated seniority list, he was open to scheduling a meeting to re-examine the issue.

I presented copies of the information packet received from Elise to committee members as we sat around the company conference table a few days later. "I don't agree with this letter signed by Anthony," said Darnell. "He didn't show it to me first. My name's not on it so I don't have to go along with it."

"Look ... all agreements are between two organizations: Mohawk and Workers United. Any union official who signs their name binds the whole union. Just as any member of management signing their name binds the whole company. It would be total chaos otherwise. The one thing I can promise is I'll never sign my name to anything before showing it to the committee."

"But can we believe you?"

"How can you even ask that after what we went through together during the decert?"

I asked if we needed to schedule a third step meeting for Reggie Anderson, disputing his sexual misconduct. Darnell said Reggie told him to forget it because he was looking for a new job.

"If I'd done something like that, I'd also be embarrassed to discuss it at a meeting," I said, then, glancing at my notes, asked about the roach-infested canteen. The mill chair said Orkin had been sent in and he hoped this time they got it right. Bill noted he still hadn't received the Kronos records necessary to investigate a lead person working overtime while folks in her department weren't making forty hours.

Management entered and took their seats. Justin acknowledged that Mia hadn't been fully trained as a weaver when imported from Landrum but had been working in this skilled craft for the past two years. Her husband, however, had never held a skilled position. We agreed to *interpret* the 2015 agreement by allowing Mia to retain seniority back to her company hire date, but not her husband. I told him to expect a draft of the new MOA by tomorrow.

"Speaking of MOAs," I said, "what about the Neighborhood Watch agreement?" Justin replied it had been referred to an in-house employment attorney named Arlene and he'd follow up.

I prepared a leaflet for the first shift meetings of the New Year, to be held in the library's large meeting room. It was titled ***Know Your Rights: Your Job May Depend On It***.

Part Three—Aftermath

I arrived at the Eden Library fifteen minutes early on January 17 to arrange the meeting room. I turned right at the end of a long hallway lined with community artwork and entered a large room filled with small tables and plastic chairs intended for toddlers. A woman at the front desk apologized for not telling me to turn left and I was soon standing in the Fieldcrest Room, equipped with a speaker's table and far more chairs than necessary.

Turnout was light, as expected. Southern textile employees don't attend meetings unless faced with imminent crisis. But several workers with questions about on-the-job injuries showed up. A slender woman wearing a wrist brace quietly took a seat during the first shift session. Following my presentation I asked about her wrist.

The woman introduced herself as Linda Collins. She'd worked for thirty years as a mender and was experiencing pain in her right wrist while sewing. I asked if she'd seen a doctor or filed a workers comp claim. She answered no to both, saying the brace helped her get through a shift.

Linda listened patiently as I explained the nature of repetitive motion injuries, saying this looked like a classic example. The pain wouldn't subside with time but slowly worsen until she could no longer function on her job. I offered the phone number of attorney Hank Patterson.

"I don't need no lawyer," she said, speaking courteously with a soft voice. "I just came here to get some information." It was apparent the sixty-year-old woman feared company reprisal and hoped to tough it out until retirement.

I've seen far too many strong people condemned to life with a disabled limb or back, because they didn't take their condition seriously or were afraid to make waves. I reviewed Linda's rights, wrote down Hank's number and asked Darnell to hand it to her. Linda politely thanked the mill chair and promised to call.

"I've got a better idea," I said picking up my cell phone. "I'll call his office right now. He probably won't be available but getting a message from me will put you at the front of the line."

I reached Hank's personal secretary, described the situation, and said the injured worker was with me and could provide more detail. Darnell walked across the floor and handed my phone to a wide-eyed Linda. She gingerly took it as if being handed a scorpion. This was far more than she'd bargained for. But regaining her composure, she gave an articulate account and provided contact information.

Justin emailed the next morning, attaching two executed MOAs for my signature:

> The MOA for Neighborhood Watch has been edited at the recommendation of counsel. The MOA regarding Mia and Joseph Linares' seniority is exactly as you had written. Please let me know if you have questions. If you are agreeable to both documents, please sign and return. Thanks.

I opened both documents and signed the first. Several lines of unnecessary verbiage had been added to the Neighborhood Watch agreement. Of greater concern was the final sentence, following the commitment that discipline would not ensue from the program:

> Nothing in this document prevents the Company from ending or changing the Neighborhood Watch Program.

This was a typical company attorney's loophole: implying management could at some point implement a new version of the program that included discipline. After cussing under my breath, I countered by writing we'd accept the new version if yet another sentence was added:

> The above statement of intent regarding information provided to management not resulting in discipline will apply to any changed version of the Neighborhood Watch Program.

Jeff and I toured the plant on January 23, accompanied by Alan Cox and another member of management. Alan was the department head who'd told security to call law enforcement if committee members conducted union business in the parking lot. I remained touched by how fondly many of the workers greeted me. I shook hands with a mender who hadn't been a witness and never attended meetings. She held onto my hand and smiled. "Please don't tell me you're going to be leaving us soon."

"No, I'll be sticking around ... at least for awhile."

"Come on, we need to keep moving," said Alan.

We were halfway through Weaving when Alan stopped in his tracks and announced, "The hour's up. Tour's over. We got to head back upstairs."

I walked calmly over and, standing two feet away, stared into his eyes.

"We're not finished. My deal with Justin is we get to stay until shift change, if necessary."

"Well, not today. I've got work to do. Let's get going."

"Well this is *my* work. I didn't drive here from out of town to walk around for an hour. My deal isn't with you. It's with the person you work for. You really don't want to be responsible for the union filing new NLRB charges against the company."

I stepped back to allow Alan a few minutes to confer with his colleague who'd been on previous tours. We resumed our visit without further interruption. A union organizer must always be prepared to turn on a dime and fight when least expected. Backing down in front of workers is never an option.

I called Justin to inform him Bill still hadn't received the Kronos records necessary to investigate work distribution in Aviation. He promised to get with Elise but assured me the lead person was no longer working hours belonging to the bargaining unit. He then asked to share something important that needed to remain temporarily confidential.

Justin had been promoted to a corporate position, though his successor had not yet been named. He would continue living in Eden and maintain an office at the plant, staying involved in collective bargaining during the transition. We hung up and I contemplated his disturbing news. The days when plant managers spent their career at one facility were long past. Within several years they were usually promoted or fired. I'd been through countless changes in plant leadership: saying an unexpected farewell to someone with whom a working relationship and level of trust had been established, then awaiting the unknown.

The situation is especially challenging when the new manager comes from a nonunion environment, accustomed to enjoying full discretion at all times. It often takes months to make him realize the contract supersedes his authority and it would be in his best interests to stop taking it personally.

On February 7, the parties held a labor management meeting. Justin said the rug business was doing poorly, commercial and residential carpets were profitable, while Aviation was flat. Overall, the business remained in the red.

The safety shirts had been postponed for several weeks and we discussed employee meetings to announce the program, with committee members present at each. I pushed for the Neighborhood Watch agreement to be finalized, knowing this would become more difficult once Justin was gone.

As committee members headed back to their departments, Justin asked me to stay behind. The company was leaning toward promoting Daphne Little to safety coordinator but he wanted my opinion. Daphne would be attending and sometimes facilitating the joint safety meetings required by contract. Justin was concerned about whether committee members could work with her and feared renewed confrontation.

I assured him we wouldn't stand in the way of anyone with an opportunity to advance themselves. I'd recommend the committee consider the war over and get along with her. Privately I thought: *That puts Daphne out of the bargaining unit and she'll no longer be entitled to sponsor a new petition. Right to Work will lose its hook in our local and move on to corrupt the process elsewhere.*

CHAPTER 20

A Barrage of New Issues

There was little need for my involvement during the next few weeks, apart from routine phone calls and emails. A reciprocal relationship was evolving between the union and company, and management was going out of its way to follow the contract.

Justin notified me Greg Lovitt had been promoted to plant manager. I felt a wave of relief pass over me as the worst-case scenarios dissipated. I instinctively liked Greg and though he would be in for a far greater transition than imagined, believed he could wrap his mind around collective bargaining and become someone the union could work with.

I told Justin my counterproposal to the Neighborhood Watch memorandum remained unanswered. This remained a priority issue. If Justin's across-the table promise went undocumented, discipline resulting from co-workers reporting each other was inevitable.

I remained in touch with Hank Patterson, delighted he was actively representing both Jessie and Linda in their workers comp claims. Inspired by the experiences of these women, I wrote a leaflet titled *REPETITIVE MOTION INJURIES*.

> Many textile jobs require you to use the *same body parts over and over,* doing the *same thing*, each day. Over the years your wrist, shoulder, back, and other places can wear out and begin to hurt.
>
> If you ignore this, it *won't get better*. It will keep getting *worse and worse*. You will pass the *point of no return* and end up disabled. If you deal with it in time, you'll probably be OK.

It concluded with a new cartoon by Patricia, depicting a mender working in pain.

On February 28, Greg Lovitt forwarded Arlene's latest version of the Neighborhood Watch agreement, concluding with:

> It is understood that the Company will notify the union if any revised version of the Program does not incorporate the non-punitive language similar to that stated here-in.

I cussed under my breath, noting my good-faith effort at compromise had been met with an even more onerous response. *It's like saying, "I agree to pay you $100 but will notify you if I change my mind."*

I called Justin as he'd been party to the understanding. "I know it's not your doing, but Arlene is making you look like a liar. She strikes me as someone with no experience in collective bargaining. Why don't you run this by Ed Cheroff?"

I felt fairly certain about the type of employment law practiced by the in-house counsel of an otherwise nonunion corporation. She defended her client against the type of claims employees can file in any environment: workers comp, discrimination based on race or gender, etc. This was probably her first fledgling attempt at reaching settlement with a union.

The committee and I met with Greg at his request during the first week in March. I shook the new plant manager's hand, offering congratulations on his promotion. He thanked me then rolled his eyes upward muttering, "Please pray for me."

Greg said he'd invited the committee to meet before making employee announcements about something important. Paul DeCock, Mohawk's new president of its Flooring North America division, was re-evaluating efficiency models. He'd determined that whenever possible, specific operations should be combined within one facility. The corporate office had decided to consolidate inventory storage at their Calhoun plant.

Karastan would be phasing out Finishing and Rug Fabrication, departments at the final stage of production that prepared product for warehousing. During the next several months, employees in both areas would be laid off, along with several people in other departments. I asked how many workers would be affected and Greg answered, "Thirty-two jobs are being eliminated. The number of layoffs will be slightly less due to attrition."

Layoffs at union plants are a complex, time-consuming proposition that guarantees maximum fairness during an otherwise tragic event. Strict seniority language governs who will be laid off. Displaced workers are entitled to *bump* less senior employees, first within their department and then elsewhere. Employees ultimately sent out are placed on *recall* status for a year. Newly available positions are filled by senior/qualified people on the list. It's an emotional time, fraught with issues over how convoluted seniority protocols should be applied to specific situations.

There is no area that varies more between union contracts than layoff/recall language. The Mohawk contract states:

As the result of a layoff:
1. If employee is displaced from their job classification in which they hold seniority then the employee can exercise bumping rights to displace the least senior employee within their own job classification, shift of their choice.
2. If the employee does not hold enough seniority in order to stay in their own job classification, then they will have the option to exercise their bumping rights to displace the least senior employee in a previously held job.
3. If the employee does not have a previously held job and they have less than two Active Written Warnings, then they will have the option to displace the least senior employee within their department until all moves are exhausted.

Arrangements were made for committee members to be present at all employee meetings, and at discussions between workers and Elise regarding their bumping options.

A few days later, I was contacted by attorney Ed Cheroff, saying the company was willing to offer a choice of two voluntary retirement incentives. We scheduled an appointment to negotiate the details. Local management would postpone announcing the layoff but time was short and we needed to agree quickly. I was favorably surprised. There was no severance language in the contract and this isn't a mandatory subject of bargaining, unless layoffs exceed one-third of the workforce.

Chapter 20. A Barrage of New Issues

During the next several days, Ed and I amended and elaborated upon provisions in both versions of the incentive: one where benefits were staggered by seniority and another where a lesser amount remained constant. The lawyer shared that buyouts of this nature weren't offered in other Mohawk plants. The company was clearly recognizing the value of labor peace.

The committee and I took our usual seats in the library conference room on March 18 to review our options. The local officers accepted that due to limited time and no actual bargaining requirement, I'd been obliged to work things out over the phone. Following an hour of heated debate, they chose the version favoring seniority. Employees with over fifteen years' service would be offered three months of pay and six months of medical insurance if they chose early retirement. The amounts decreased with tenure.

The memorandum also stated:

> Employees will have fourteen days, beginning on the ratification of this proposal, to decide whether to opt for this incentive.
>
> Employees who opt for this incentive will be expected to enter into a severance agreement and general release, and will relinquish all seniority rights effective the date of their separation.

Jeff noted that Daphne was all over the plant in her new position as safety coordinator, talking with workers and participating in departmental meetings. Darnell vowed to "get in her face" and make her life miserable at every safety meeting.

"How will that help our members?" I asked. "You've got to learn to see the big picture and think tactically. Who would you rather be dealing with: Daphne in a safety meeting or Right to Work down the road?"

We reconvened with Greg on March 21 to execute the retirement incentive and schedule employee meetings. After Greg left the room, I asked committee members to urge Fabrication and Finishing employees who lacked bumping opportunities to take the package, because they'd be leaving anyway. Though unfortunate, these events underscored the value of the union having survived a decertification petition circulated by low-seniority workers.

I wrote a leaflet scheduling shift meetings to discuss the layoff:

BE GRATEFUL
FOR YOUR UNION CONTRACT

> In every other Mohawk plant, the Company decides who stays and who goes during a layoff. If management doesn't like you, or would simply prefer someone younger ... you're out the door! Your years of service mean nothing.

Part Three—Aftermath

But under our union contract: **SENIORITY = JOB SECURITY**. You can't be forced out because of favoritism. That's worth its weight in gold in today's unstable world.

Under our union contract: management still has rules but *workers have rights*.

A few days later, Jeff called to inform me a journalist from *Rockingham Now* had gotten wind of the layoff. The local president had referred her to me for comment. Shortly afterward, my phone rang and I gave the interview to reporter Susie C. Spear. I focused my remarks on the importance of a union contract when jobs are at stake. Susie said she'd be contacting Jeff and asked for phone numbers of other local officers who could provide a worker's perspective. She reached Bill and he offered some thoughtful quotes:

Right now I think everybody is still in a little bit of shock about it. There's really not a clear picture of how everything is going to go, yet.

The article ran two days later and Jeff called that morning. "People talking all over the plant about why Bill got interviewed and not me. I'm the president. I'm the one supposed to be doing the interviews."

I tried to explain that I had no control over who a reporter interviewed and what they printed, but Jeff cut me off every few seconds, repeating his arguments. Fortunately he was at work, so the conversation ended along with his break period.

I entered the library on April 4 prepared for anything. Layoffs have generated some of the most volatile union meetings of my career. Workforce reductions inherently pit the interests of one worker against another. Drunken men occasionally show up ready to fight to the death over jobs that contractually belong to someone else.

More seats were filled than any meeting since the decert, but the group was polite and orderly. There were numerous questions but members expressed gratitude for their jobs having been protected by the contract.

The local president was back in good spirits. After the final meeting he turned toward me. "Have you heard that Robin Stone got laid off from Quality Control?" I replied no and he continued. "She was up in there with three other girls, all of them with just a couple of years seniority. Robin been with the company over twenty years but they let her go without giving her a reason. She went around the plant saying, 'How could they do me like this after all I done for them?'"

As a *nonbargaining unit employee*, Robin wasn't covered by the

Chapter 20. A Barrage of New Issues

contract. In my experience, decertification sponsors are usually treated like management darlings until the effort fails, at which point they find themselves expendable. This example clearly demonstrated how little Mohawk prioritized seniority unless required to do so.

The following week, Greg requested a meeting to review changes in corporate disability benefits. The conference room was in use so the committee and I were directed to the showroom. Shortly after we took our seats, Leslie Taylor walked through the door. This was the first time I'd seen her in months but her presence made sense, as we were discussing a company-wide program. I rose to shake her hand and we met halfway between the entrance and conference table. Something seemed off about her demeanor, as though she was trying to switch on her inner light but it only flickered. Her face appeared weary and the customary smiles weren't at the ready.

"How have you been?" I politely asked.

"I'm retiring and moving back to Tennessee."

I remained behind with the committee following a short and routine discussion. I asked the local officers if they'd noticed anything different about Leslie. Darnell and Bill commented she seemed a bit distracted.

"I don't believe her retirement was voluntary," I said. "I think she was forced out because of how the decert ended up. Remember what I said at the very beginning. Companies have zero tolerance for failure. It must have been an awful experience, having to return here during her final days to meet with us."

Darnell called from work regarding a senior union member in Rug Fabrication named Clay Willis. The mill chair was more upset about this issue than I'd heard him in a long time. Clay had taken the retirement package, having been told by management and the union his entire department was shutting. Though in his early sixties, he'd remained in the department his whole life and therefore lacked bumping rights back to a former job.

Shorty after the fourteen-day window closed, Clay noticed two lift operator positions posted for bids. The lifts had only run part time on a fill-in basis for the past year but were listed as part of Rug Fabrication on seniority reports. The senior employee could have easily claimed one of these jobs if made aware his department wasn't fully closing.

On May 2, the committee and I met with Greg and Elise to discuss this unexpected issue. Greg had obviously been briefed, arguing Clay signed a binding contract and exceptions couldn't be made without opening the door to a floodgate of other employees with demands. "We have to treat everyone the same," he concluded.

I noted that while the union obviously agreed with the principle of equal treatment, this was an unusual situation. Clay had opted for the package in good faith, based upon the information provided. In fact, his supervisor had told employees the department was being discontinued during a start-up meeting. I proposed a *non precedent* memorandum of agreement, allowing him to decline the incentive but not guaranteeing any specific job.

"That protects you from further employee claims. Clay understands that in the unlikely event he doesn't get one of the lift jobs, he's out of luck and gets laid off without benefits."

Elise asserted that Rug Fabrication *had completely shut* and that the full-time lift positions were being reinstated as part of a Warehouse skeleton crew. I characterized the timing as suspect and said the jobs should have remained in Fabrication during the transition to avoid confusion.

Greg seemed open-minded but had to consult with corporate. The committee departed feeling cautiously optimistic. He handed me yet another draft of the Neighborhood Watch agreement. The language no longer blatantly reserved management's right to change its mind, but still contained loopholes Justin never intended.

That evening I drafted one more counterproposal, going out of my way to reassure Mohawk on all fronts except the option to back out of the primary agreement. This simplest of all understandings was evolving into a piece of legislation:

> The above statement of intent regarding information provided to management not resulting in discipline of bargaining unit members will apply to any changed version of the "Neighborhood Watch" Program at the Eden facility although nothing in this document shall be used as precedent to limit the company's ability to implement other safety programs.

The plant manager followed up two days later regarding Clay Willis. Company lawyers refused to grant exceptions to signed contracts. I decided to go directly to the source and called Ed Cheroff. We held a series of animated discussions over the next two weeks. I took my stand on a legal principle rendering contracts invalid, if signed based on fraudulent representations. Ed said management hadn't engaged in deliberate misrepresentation. Employees were told the building was in a realignment process and the final outcome couldn't be guaranteed.

Chapter 20. A Barrage of New Issues

Ed couldn't be persuaded on legal or ethical grounds and became increasingly frustrated with me for continuing to push the issue. I told him that following weeks of discussion at our level, the grievance process would be a waste of time and I'd be filing for arbitration. He said the employer would first want a third step hearing to get all positions on record.

Patricia and I drove to Atlanta on June 1 for the annual Southern Region convention. An accident on I-85 in South Carolina stopped traffic for an hour then forced us into a detour without signs directing traffic back to the highway. The area was so remote even the GPS was confused, sending us on long circular journeys back to our starting point. It took two hours of trial and error to finally return to the interstate.

The next day I had a long meeting with Harris and Mike about Clay Willis. I have full discretion regarding all matters in the field except arbitration, because of the cost. If our union litigated every sympathetic case lacking solid legal foundation, we'd go bankrupt. The final analysis was management's misrepresentations did not rise to the level of willful fraud and therefore didn't compromise their right to enforce the early retirement contract.

I met with committee members to provide an honest account of the Atlanta discussion, relieved they all took it philosophically and understood my hands were tied. I pointed out that losing an arbitration would tarnish our image of invincibility and guarantee we'd seen the end of retirement incentives. However, Clay was entitled to a third step hearing and one was scheduled for June 19.

"Don't tell them we don't plan to arbitrate until you get their answer," said Darnell. "Maybe you can still back them down."

I returned to Eden a week later to prep with Clay Willis and local officers in the plant conference room. The grievant was a short, slender black man with a calm disposition. I suggested he not get his hopes up because the company's legal position was insurmountable but promised my best efforts.

He surprised me by saying, "I never really expected to win. I know I signed a contract. I just wanted a chance to have my say before leaving."

I realized all the emotion regarding this issue had come from committee members.

Greg and Elise entered the room, followed by an attractive woman with shoulder length hair dressed business casual. She sat immediately to Greg's right. Elise introduced Claire Mathews, the new corporate Human Resource director. I'd never encountered anyone so young in such a lofty position.

I was a passionate advocate on Clay's behalf and allowed him time to express his feelings. Claire quietly observed, taking in every nuance, but didn't participate. I sensed none of the hubris or bias often found in corporate directors. The union proposed a settlement whereby the grievant would forfeit both his severance and bumping rights but be granted the first open job to become available.

Following the grievance meeting, Greg discussed the corporate smoking policy that would soon be implemented in Eden. The penalty for smoking on company property was currently a ten-day suspension. Following employee meetings to be held within a few days, the first offense would result in discharge. I raised just cause concerns, making eye contact with the new Human Resource executive.

I stayed behind to become better acquainted with Claire Mathews. She'd previously been the Human Resource manager at a union plant in Illinois and clearly had no axes to grind. A management transition of this nature is a frequent consequence of failed decertifications: replacing an anti-union executive with someone comfortable in collective bargaining environments.

Ten days later I received the expected denial of Clay Willis' grievance. Having been handed the proverbial lemon, I decided to at least make some lemonade. I called Greg and told him the union planned to withdraw the arbitration but expected one thing in return: a signed copy of my recently revised Neighborhood Watch memorandum, exactly as written. Forty-eight hours later I had it.

I emailed the union's position statement regarding smoking policy to Greg and Claire:

- A corporate policy doesn't supersede the union contract.
- Our contract states that discipline can only be for just cause, thereby invoking the Just Cause Doctrine.
- One of the seven tests of the Just Cause Doctrine is that punishment must fit the crime.
- Automatic discharge for the first violation of a smoking policy is unreasonable and in violation of just cause.
- There are various circumstances under which an employee can be caught violating a smoking policy, ranging from smoking while operating heavy equipment to smoking outside the building while on break.
- In the event an employee is discharged for a first offense of the smoking policy, the union will evaluate the circumstances, and reserves its right to grieve and arbitrate.

Chapter 20. A Barrage of New Issues

Over the next several weeks, the collective bargaining relationship continued its slow transformation back toward normal. When informed by committee members of unjust or excessive discipline, it usually took only a phone call to have the matter quickly resolved. When Jeff and I toured the plant, we were greeted with expressions of gratitude from senior workers who rightly credited the contract for protecting their jobs during the layoff. Unfortunately, it was difficult to translate this into membership. Otherwise supportive nonmembers had watched the greatest union victory in their recollection unfold the previous year and enjoyed job security during the layoff without signing a card. Ironically, the membership drive was being hampered by our success. That's the singular intent behind right-to-work laws—weakening unions by appealing to the human potential for selfishness.

Greg requested another LMC on July 23 to review the cell phone policy being revised in all plants. Employers understandably resent the ongoing distraction posed by portable phones. They don't want workers looking away from machines to answer texts. I'd had this discussion at countless facilities.

The new plant manager said going forward, employees would be written up if caught looking at their phone during working hours. I countered with the union's primary concern at all our facilities: single parents with small children in daycare and workers with sick family members needed to remain available. One might consider this a simple exercise in common sense but it usually takes a union to raise and enforce the principle.

Following an hour of debate, Greg agreed that employees could keep their phones on vibrate to monitor calls and texts. If legitimate emergencies required a response, they'd exit the manufacturing area for safety reasons. I asked where things stood with the smoking policy. Greg confided he'd received an email from Arlene instructing him to maintain the current policy at our plant for legal reasons.

Local officers joined me at the library the following week for what I assumed would be a routine follow-up meeting and opportunity to plan another picnic. We reviewed the union's recent accomplishments and the importance of workers knowing whom to thank. Thomas remained silent and hunched over until we were finished, then looked up and said, "I want to discuss my grievance about the write-up I got last month."

He described a pre-shift meeting held outside the Weave Room canteen by supervisor Gil Norman. Thomas had been running late and didn't have time to get an orange safety vest from his locker. Gil shouted, "You gotta leave! You ain't got no vest on."

Thomas said he was so upset by being spoken to this way in front of co-workers that he avoided pre-shift meetings for the next three days and was ultimately written up. The first two steps of his grievance were denied. His deeply emotional account lasted for an hour. He seemed far more concerned about having been publicly disrespected than disciplined. The vice mill chair provided examples of other employees who'd been reprimanded by Gil Norman in the presence of others.

My instincts told me to tread lightly but with honesty. Thomas seemed to have cast light on the type of supervisor misconduct not tolerated in union plants. I felt it would be useful to expose this in a third step forum but the grievance itself was unwinnable. New union stewards are always taught a simple rule of thumb: *Obey now. Grieve later.*

"That's ok," said Thomas. "I'm willing to be the sacrificial lamb if it puts a stop to people being treated this way. If a supervisor got a problem with someone, they should discuss it in private, in their office."

The parties met on August 7 for Thomas Meadors' third step grievance. Claire Mathews had flown from Calhoun as the corporate representative. I provided an outline of events leading to discipline and turned the floor over to the vice mill chair. Thomas sat on the far end of the union's side of the table, wearing an orange safety vest over his maintenance uniform, with an orange ball cap turned backwards.

There was no difference of opinion regarding the morning that set things in motion: Thomas had been thrown out of a pre-shift meeting for not wearing his safety vest. He'd subsequently failed to attend meetings for the next three days, finally resulting in a write-up for *negligence*. Thomas felt the rude treatment justified abstaining from several meetings, noting he was allowing for a cooling-off period between him and the supervisor, to avoid escalating conflict. He offered examples of other employees being publicly humiliated by Gil Norman.

Greg promised to counsel the supervisor regarding professional interaction with workers and agreed criticism should always be offered in private. He didn't dispute the local officer's claim to being offended but said it didn't justify subsequent conduct that could have been deemed insubordinate.

"Let me tell you something," said Thomas. "It doesn't matter much now because I'm sixty-five years old and this happened when I was nineteen. A supervisor treated me wrong and I waited for him in the parking lot with a gun but he never showed up. I'm a church-going man now and not like that anymore, but I still believe in keeping distance from someone when I'm upset."

Greg remained composed and suggested the grievant should have raised concerns with a department head, rather than engaging in further rule violations. Thomas sat upright and turned toward the plant manager. "You're nothing but a slave master sitting on his plantation."

The hearing ended shortly afterward and committee members returned to their jobs. I gathered files into my briefcase and was headed toward the exit when Greg summoned me into his office.

"I'm really upset about what just happened at the meeting," he said from behind his desk, "and need to talk with someone. I felt you'd be the best person."

I took a seat and listened. "No one's ever referred to me as a slave master. I don't know what to make of that. I thought we were trying to have a professional relationship but I guess I was wrong."

I agreed the remark was inappropriate but told him collective bargaining required a thick skin, and suggested he not take comments made in anger to heart.

"I thought I had a thick skin," he said, "but now I'm not so sure."

Greg's larger concern was that Claire left the building believing a productive relationship with us was impossible. She'd been more put off by the gun story and was worried about Thomas' rage building to the point where he shot someone.

"I've been around violent people my whole life," I said. "When there's a real potential for violence, I sense it in five seconds. I guarantee you Thomas doesn't pose a threat. He was just trying to make a legitimate point in the wrong way."

We continued speaking for an hour and I concluded by saying we were part of a relationship between two national organizations, that shouldn't be defined by the conduct of one individual on either side. The next morning I had a similar discussion with Claire and believed fences had been mended.

On August 12, 2019, the National Labor Relations Board published a Notice of Proposed Rule Making in the Federal Register to amend Part 103 of its Rules and Regulations, eliminating the *blocking charge policy*; just as Ira, Mike and NLRB field agents had feared. It is of note that rather than attempting to change policy by establishing precedent through a test case, the Board was invoking the formal rule making process described in

Ira's brief. If successful, the lengthy procedure will further strip workers of protection from employer-sponsored decertifications, legislated under Roosevelt (a president who truly helped *make America great*). The current administration is systematically reversing his accomplishments.

The Senate Committee on Health, Education, Labor, and Pensions issued a press release regarding a letter written by Senator Patty Murray to NLRB Chairman John Ring. Senator Murray objected to the proposed rule change and stated, "Workers count on the NLRB to protect their rights and they need to know the NLRB is operating in a thorough, deliberate and impartial way."

Toward the end of the month, I stopped for gas at 1:30 p.m. following a labor-management meeting and received a text from Jessie Dotson:

> I know you was meeting with the company this morning. I was wondering if you had time to meet with me. I have some serious questions to ask. You seem to take me serious. I thought meeting I could show you the paperwork I have.

I called and told her I hadn't eaten since breakfast but she was welcome to join me at Ruby Tuesday for lunch. She lived in a small town thirty miles away and I waited in the parking lot for forty-five minutes. Finally, a white truck pulled in beside me and Jessie exited, wearing a black lace top and jeans ripped at both knees. She reminded me of a Greenwich Village girl from the 1960s.

I ordered my usual turkey burger but Jessie felt uncomfortable being treated to lunch. I told her eating alone would make me "feel like a pig" and the union was paying, so she finally requested a breaded pork chop. She pulled a tablet from her purse and began deftly opening scanned documents. I realized she was probably more high-tech than me.

Jessie was on leave of absence following shoulder surgery and was still in considerable pain. She believed the amount of her weekly workers comp check was too low and worse, payments had stopped arriving weeks ago. The bank was threatening to foreclose on her house.

The formula for calculating workers comp payments is simple on its face: two thirds of average weekly earnings. However, there are numerous variables that can positively or negatively impact that amount. Jessie was only receiving $314 relative to her previous $600 paychecks. She also wasn't being reimbursed for travel expenses to physical therapy. It appeared she was being underpaid and I promised to call Hank Patterson. I reminded her that the really big money would be coming next year when she received her disability rating.

Chapter 20. A Barrage of New Issues

Jessie asked a number of other questions regarding her situation, pulling up related documents on her tablet. I'd never seen a union officer more organized in tracking a case and raising pertinent concerns.

"I should have been a lawyer," she told me.

"What you could be is a shop steward when you get back to work. I'll train the hell out of you, as much as you want. Once you have some experience, you might get yourself elected to the committee and sit across the table from management."

On September 4, I received an email from Greg:

I have planned a Business Meeting with you and the union leadership on Wednesday morning at 9:30 a.m. It will be held in the conference room by my office. Sorry for the late notice but it is very important for you guys to attend.

The next morning we learned that Paul DeCock had taken another step in consolidating domestic operations. Mohawk was ceasing production of Karastan's iconic woolen rugs. The marketplace no longer supported their existence. All synthetic rug manufacturing would take place in Georgia. The Eden plant would focus entirely on its areas with the highest profit potential: residential and commercial carpeting. New products were under development that senior management believed would be profitable by June 2020. As a result, twenty more jobs were scheduled for elimination: weavers on affected looms and their support staff, ranging from creelers to fixers.

I asked if management would be offering another early retirement incentive. Greg and Claire both shook their heads. On impulse, I asked if the company would reconsider if we agreed to not file grievances regarding its application. Claire said she'd take the proposal back to Calhoun.

Several meetings ensued as the parties hashed out differences regarding the boundaries between different job classifications. To my surprise, another incentive package was authorized.

During October, I received an updated seniority list. The bargaining unit stood at ninety-five employees and our membership had reached majority status. The two layoffs had mainly eliminated employees hired three years before, who'd never supported the union and in some cases sought its decertification. Their efforts to supplant the senior workers who remained had failed.

Jessie's workers comp payments were increased to their full amount and the shortfall was paid in a lump sum. She kept her house. The supervisor abuses brought to light by Thomas' colorful grievance were curtailed. Since the second layoff, all has remained quiet on the Eden front, but 2020 will no doubt offer new surprises.

There's one thing I'm certain of. The decertification did not originate at the Karastan plant in Eden. The scheme was hatched at a corporate level and implemented through its Human Resource division. I wasn't able to prove all of this but it didn't matter. We documented management's illegal involvement far more than was necessary.

I must express gratitude to Fredrick Englehart for creating transcripts of my radio interviews and publishing them in his briefs. They were of absolutely no value to his case but proved a useful resource while writing this book.

Index

Index